The Toddler's Science Activity Book

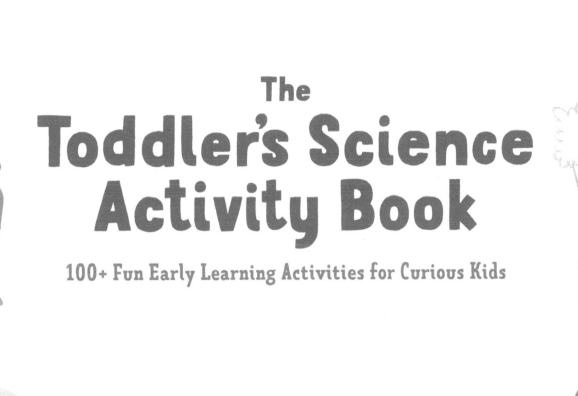

The Toddler's Science Activity Book

100+ Fun Early Learning Activities for Curious Kids

Kailan Carr

Illustrations by Natascha Rosenberg

ROCKRIDGE
PRESS

Series Designer: Suzanne LaGasa
Interior and Cover Designer: Jennifer Hsu
Art Producer: Tom Hood
Editor: Mary Colgan
Production Editor: Nora Milman

Illustrations © Natascha Rosenberg, 2021. Photographs Adene Sanchez/iStock, p. ii; Shutterstock, pp. xii, 15, 68, 94; DragonImages/iStock, p. 16; VioletaStoimenova/iStock, p. 42; michellegibson/iStock, p. 120; SDI Productions/iStock, p. 148. Author photograph courtesy Lando Lane Creative.

ISBN: Print 978-1-64876-643-5 | eBook 978-1-64876-145-4
R1

To my kids,
who are my inspiration for
learning through play!

Contents

CHAPTER 4: **Touch and Feel 69**

CHAPTER 5: **Rainbow Science 95**

CHAPTER 6: **Wonder of Water 121**

- 1 -
PLAY AND LEARN

Toddlers have a natural curiosity. I remember what a thrill it was as a parent to see the world through their eyes. Their excitement about everyday occurrences is infectious. Who knew seeing an airplane in the sky would be exciting again, or that watching a bug crawl on a leaf would inspire newfound awe?

This is why the first three years of your child's life present the perfect opportunity to encourage an interest in science. They are learning new things about the world around them every day. Every hour even! Toddlers soak up new information and experiences, so let's support them in their daily learning with simple science activities.

The activities in this book are designed to delight toddlers, inspire learning through play, and introduce a range of science skills in a fun, age-appropriate way!

My Toddler-Parenting Science Adventure

My kids were born at the same time as the iPad. As the newest, coolest thing, it quickly ended up in toddlers' hands everywhere (my children included). I witnessed how the devices took over their minds as they tuned out the world, and I endured the tantrums or whining when it was time to put them away.

It didn't take long for me to say "No more." One day, the battery died. I put the iPad in a drawer and there it stayed through their preschool years. What did we do instead? We played! My husband was a junior high science teacher at the time and I taught early elementary school before I stayed home with my kids. I thoroughly enjoyed setting up these activities and watching my children investigate and explore. That's what science is about!

The good news is that we still enjoy doing these same things together now—and my kids are six and eight years old! Keep this book around, because these activities will grow with your child.

I know days with toddlers can be long and draining. It takes extra effort to keep them busy without a device. I've been there. But I'm coming at you from the other side. I want to tell you that it is 1,000 percent worth it. You are giving them the tools they need to be creative kids who don't need to rely on devices to be entertained. My kids were under stay-at-home orders during a pandemic for 60-plus days and always found something to do. They wrote stories, read books, built forts, cooked using recipes, drew pictures, built with plastic construction blocks, and practiced piano. I believe the limited screen time in their early years helped them become more creatively independent children.

Benefits of Science Play

Did you know that 80 percent of a child's brain is developed by age three? A baby is born with all the neurons they will have for life. Skills develop by making connections between those neurons. How does this happen? Any time you read, sing, or play with your child, you are helping them form these neural connections. This is called a serve and return relationship—one where you interact back and forth.

The Center on the Developing Child at Harvard University writes, "Early experiences affect the quality of that architecture by establishing either a sturdy or a fragile foundation for all of the learning, health, and behavior that follow."

In the journal *Pediatrics*, the authors of a study wrote, "Play is not frivolous; it is brain building. Play has been shown to have both direct and indirect effects on brain structure and functioning."

Parents, you have a vital role in supporting your child's learning and development. Doing science activities together is a great way to encourage back-and-forth conversation by asking questions and observing outcomes. You will also bond with your child and inspire a love for science that leads to lasting curiosity and critical thinking.

Toddler Time

This book contains real science demonstrations, some of which you may remember from your school days. Why are we doing them with toddlers? Because it's fun to watch and explore! We don't expect children at this age to get scientific or understand the explanations behind what's happening.

The goal is exposure. The goal is to encourage observation and questioning and to connect with your child and instill a love for science. The neat thing is that you can go back to these activities when they are older and go a little more in-depth about the science behind them!

There are also several activities where your toddler will get to jump in and take the lead. They will explore new sensations, take a closer look at nature around them, and practice fine motor skills.

Every child develops at their own pace and will be ready for different activities in their own time. But let's take a look at development milestones to get a general idea of how toddlers progress. It's amazing how much they grow in such a short time!

12 to 18 Months

The rapid physical growth of infancy starts to slow as babies reach their first birthday and move into toddlerhood. The focus shifts to how their bodies interact in space and the world around them while they work on mastering new skills. Here are some specific skills that start emerging:

Gross Motor Skills:

- Stands without support
- Walks with few falls
- Squats to pick something up
- Sits independently on a chair
- Climbs stairs or furniture
- Tosses a ball underhand while seated

Fine Motor Skills:

- Claps their hands
- Waves goodbye
- Holds a crayon and scribbles
- Uses fingertips to pick up small objects
- Drinks from a cup
- Uses a spoon
- Scoops materials for play
- Stacks a couple of objects
- Bangs objects together

Language and Social-Emotional Skills:

- Continues babbling
- May use 5 to 10 words
- Points at familiar people and objects in pictures
- Imitates others during play
- Can identify a couple of body parts
- Shakes head to respond to yes/no questions
- Follows simple directions
- Has an interest in interacting with people
- Can locate objects pointed to
- Turns head in response to hearing their name

18 to 24 Months

As toddlers approach their second birthday, social and play skills expand. While they still primarily imitate during play, they start to interact more with others and even delve into some pretend play, too. Here are some specific skills they often exhibit:

Gross Motor Skills:

- Walks and runs
- Coordinates movements for play
- Jumps with feet together
- Walks up and down stairs
- Throws a ball into a box
- Uses ride-on toys

Fine Motor Skills:

- Uses fingers and thumb to hold a crayon
- Opens containers
- Turns the pages of a book
- Scribble-writes with writing tools
- Builds with four or more blocks
- Turns over and pours out contents of containers

Language and Social-Emotional Skills:

- Starts to use two-word phrases
- Can name objects in pictures
- Understands action words
- Starts to use pronouns (you, my, me)
- Can identify three to five body parts
- Follows simple two-step directions
- Interacts with others during play
- May play with toys without mouthing them
- Enjoys directing play

24 to 36 Months

After toddlers turn two years old, their cognitive, language, and social-emotional learning take center stage over the previous year's focus on physical development. That social-emotional growth brings with it toddlers' desire for more independence, too, though. That—combined with expanding language skills helping them communicate their wants (and their "NO!"s)—can prove to be quite challenging. Here are the important skills they're developing:

Gross Motor Skills:

- Kicks a ball forward
- Can stand on tiptoes
- Pulls toys behind while walking
- Carries large toys while walking
- Can ride a tricycle
- Catches a large ball
- Jumps over an object
- Walks along a balance beam

Fine Motor Skills:

- Uses a pincer grasp to pick up small objects
- Turns door handles
- Screws lids on containers
- Can string large beads
- Starts to draw squares and circles

Language and Social-Emotional Skills:

- Uses two- to four-word sentences
- Talks understandably
- Demonstrates increasing independence
- Plays make-believe
- Begins to sort objects by colors and shapes
- Starts to understand "same" and "different"
- Enjoys listening to and telling stories
- Starts to count and understand numbers
- Becomes increasingly inventive during play

There are more than 100 science-based activities in this book, and each will foster several different developmental skills. The specific skills are represented by simple icons at the top of each page. You can use the icons to choose activities based on a certain skill that you want to focus on. Or perhaps you'd like to make your decision for a particular activity based on how messy it may be or how long it takes. Those variables are also listed for you to consider! There is an activity for any scenario, but no matter what, your child will be connecting with you and learning through play!

Skills Learned

 asking questions

 colors

 hand-eye coordination

 patterns

 biology

 comparing

 imagination

 physics

 botany

123 counting

 language development

 predicting

 cause and effect

 creativity

 matching

 problem-solving

 chemistry

 fine motor skills

 measuring

 sensory development

 classifying

 following directions

 observation

 shapes

 gross motor skills

 weather

Safety First!

You'll notice some activities have a note of **Caution!** Some science activities have ingredients or steps that could pose safety risks to your child if they aren't being supervised closely. Use these notes of caution to determine which activities are a good fit for your child and situation. Be sure to also follow these general safety guidelines when doing any of the activities with your toddler:

- Consider your toddler's development and abilities when choosing activities. Monitor and assist as needed when trying advanced activities.

- Avoid activities with small materials or ingredients that are not taste-safe if your toddler mouths objects during play.

- Always supervise closely when cooking with your child.

- Always supervise closely during water play and never leave bins, buckets, or pools of water unattended.

- Always check the temperature of hot water or mixtures before allowing your child to play.

- Keep your toddler away from sharp scissors, knives, mixers, hot glue guns, and other potentially hazardous tools. If possible, do any prep requiring these tools when your toddler is napping or not present.

- Whenever possible, choose nontoxic, kid-friendly art supplies and materials. If a material is new to you and likely to come in contact with your toddler's skin, test it on a small area before play.

- Always use sunscreen during outdoor play, and remember to reapply after water play and according to the package directions.

- Always check your child for rashes, skin irritations, and ticks after outdoor play, especially when playing in tall grasses or new areas.

- Some science setups could pose tripping, slipping, falling, choking, and strangulation hazards if kids are left unsupervised. Take down and put away all play setups after play has ended.

All the activities are designed for your toddler and you. Always supervise during play.

How to Use This Book

My hope for this book is that it inspires you to introduce your toddler to science through play. It will give you the tools to encourage your child to problem-solve and ask questions. As you explore together, you will connect with your child and create a lifelong interest in science! Here are some tips for using this book:

Use what you have. The activities in this book are divided into five categories that all have minimal material requirements: nature play, mix it up, touch and feel, rainbow science, and wonder of water. You will likely find most materials around your house. They include basic pantry items, your child's toys, or kitchen items. I encourage you to choose reusable items whenever you can. If you use plastic, rinse it out and save it for another activity!

Keep the essentials handy. It's a good idea to stock up on some dedicated items for your child's science investigation through play. Use a large storage container or box to hold muffin pans, a pitcher, measuring cups, a funnel, tweezers or tongs, a pipette or turkey baster, jars, spoons, etc. Some consumable items that are always good to have on hand for science play are food coloring, baking soda, vinegar, shaving cream, flour, oil, glue, rice, ice, and paint!

Look past the mess. Some days you just don't have it in you to do something messy that you have to clean. I get it. But the benefits your child gets from engaging in messy play outweigh the time it takes to clean up. Focus on the learning. Don't do messy activities if it will just stress you out and prevent you from enjoying that time with your child. But bring on the mess on days when you need to clean anyway or can take the activity outside. Each activity includes a messiness rating ranging from one to five, so you can look for that to plan ahead. You can also keep a bucket of clean water next to your child so they can rinse their hands and start over if they'd like. Lastly, lay out a sheet or towel under a messy activity so you can easily pick it up and shake it off or wash it.

Get outside when you can. We often spend too much time indoors. It's important for children to get outside every day. Let the sun touch their skin and fresh air fill their lungs. It's a proven mood booster! Many activities in this book can be done indoors or outdoors, so when you have the choice, opt to go outside!

Don't try to do it all. There are more than 100 activities in this book! Don't wear yourself out. Go through the pages and choose activities from each section that you think your child will enjoy and be able to do. A year from now, those choices will probably be different! Keep the book handy, because there are plenty of options that you can set up in a pinch when the mood strikes you both.

Consider your toddler's interests. Everyone is more excited or curious about an activity when it's something they are interested in. Choose activities based on what your child is loving at the moment. Are they into bugs? Do something from the nature chapter. Do they like to help you cook? Pick an activity from the Mix It Up chapter. It's also good to try something new every so often, because you never know what may become your child's new interest!

Consider your toddler's attention span and time of day. Toddlers' attention spans are short. The activities in this book all include a time estimate ranging from 5 to 30 minutes. Choose an activity that best fits your toddler's attention span and mood. You probably don't want to start an activity when it's almost nap time or when they are hungry.

Use the activities as a starting point. One of the things I love most about open-ended play is watching where my kids take the activity next. Their imaginations and creativity just soar. For example, a five-minute activity on static electricity may turn into a game of "Don't let the balloon touch the floor." Encourage any and all extended play! Once they get going, you may even be able to step back as they practice playing independently.

It's okay if something doesn't work right. Not every activity will turn out as you expect. I've tried to be as detailed as possible in the instructions, but sometimes an activity may take some trial and error. Use unexpected results as learning opportunities with your child and discuss the scientific process. When something doesn't work out, take note and try again!

Ultimately, remember to focus on the fun and play while introducing your child to the world of science. Enjoy watching them learn and explore!

- 2 -
NATURE PLAY

Kids spend significantly more time indoors these days than the previous generation did. Taking your toddler outside to play is important! Make it a daily routine and your child will grow to appreciate nature and all that it gives us.

Being outside is good for the mind and body. Did you know that being around greenery can counteract the negative effects of screen time on kids? It reduces stress and anxiety, increases creativity, and gets them moving!

Nature is the perfect classroom. These activities will help your child connect to nature and observe their surroundings, which is a very important scientific skill! They will also learn cause and effect, learn how to classify objects, and practice fine motor skills—all while engaging in plenty of sensory play and language development.

SKILLS
LEARNED

fine motor
skills

problem-
solving

sensory
development

botany

matching

Nature Shape Puzzle

This activity requires little ones to carefully look for the similarities and differences between objects in nature.

Messiness: 1
Prep time: None
Activity time: 10 minutes

MATERIALS

Items from nature, such as various rocks, sticks, leaves, flowers, and pine cones

Sheets of paper (or a large piece of butcher paper)

Marker

STEPS

1. Head outside and look for four or more natural items with your toddler.

2. Trace the items on the paper with your marker to create a shape puzzle.

3. Ask your child to put each nature item on top of the outline that it matches to complete the puzzle.

TIP *For younger children, keep it simple with a few objects that are obviously different (e.g., rock, stick, leaf). If the child is older, gather objects that are similar but vary in size and shape (e.g., smaller rock, medium rock, large rock, etc.).*

CAUTION! *Take care not to pick items like small rocks that could be choking hazards. Be aware of any sticks with sharp points. Avoid picking berries. Some are poisonous!*

Nature Hairstyles

Will it be a pine needle spike up or a leafy bob? Gather different natural materials and arrange them in different hairstyles on paper heads.

Messiness: 1
Prep time: 5 minutes
Activity time: 10 minutes

MATERIALS

Sheets of paper
(or a large piece of
butcher paper)

Marker

Items from nature,
such as sticks, leaves,
and flowers

Glue (optional)

PREP

Draw a large head and face on a piece of paper and leave the hair off. Draw several heads if you want to glue down the materials and have multiple people.

STEPS

1. Go on a walk around your yard or a public area to collect some items from nature.

2. Invite your child to arrange your collections on the head to make hair. It's silly and fun! You can glue your natural materials down or leave them loose to change out the hairstyles.

CAUTION! *Take care not to pick items like small rocks that could be choking hazards. Be aware of any sticks with sharp points. Avoid picking berries. Some are poisonous!*

Rock Towers

This activity is an exploration in physics and balance. Your little one will figure out they need a large, sturdy base, and how to stack the rocks to keep them from toppling.

Messiness: 1
Prep time: **None**
Activity time: 10 minutes

MATERIALS

An assortment
of rocks

STEPS

1. Go on a rock hunt in your yard.

2. Invite your child to stack two rocks. Ask them to experiment with what works better—a smaller rock on the bottom or a larger rock on the bottom. How about using two smaller rocks as the base?

3. Once you have a sturdy base, invite them to add another rock to make a stack of three. Then see how many they can stack before it falls!

TIP *Stacking stones has become a wildly popular activity in natural parks and on public property. This is damaging animal ecosystems and causing erosion. Please keep the rock stacking at your house!*

CAUTION! *Take care not to pick rocks that could be choking hazards. If it can fit through a toilet paper tube, find a bigger rock.*

sensory
development

creativity

imagination

SKILLS
LEARNED

Mud Cakes!

Find a muddy area or make some mud "batter" yourself by adding water to dirt. Then it's time to get baking!

Messiness: 5
Prep time: None
Activity time: 20 minutes

MATERIALS

Muddy area or dirt

Water in a squeeze bottle or cup

Sticks, spoons, or shovels

Muffin pans or pie pans

Items from nature, such as sticks, leaves, grass, and flowers

STEPS

1. Head to a muddy area or somewhere with dirt. If needed, invite your child to pour water on the dirt to make mud.

2. Ask your child to make you some mud cakes using the muffin pans or pie pans.

3. Encourage your little baker to use the items from nature as ingredients or decorations.

CAUTION! *Take care not to pick items like small rocks that could be choking hazards. Be aware of any sticks with sharp points. Avoid picking berries. Some are poisonous!*

SKILLS
LEARNED

language
development

imagination

weather

Cloud Pictures

The next time there are clouds in the sky, try this simple and fun activity. Once you introduce it, your child will be on the lookout for cloud pictures everywhere you go!

Messiness: 1
Prep time: **None**
Activity time: 5 minutes

MATERIALS

Blanket (optional)

STEPS

1. Look up at the sky. To make cloud gazing more comfortable, put a blanket on the ground to lie on (if using).

2. Tell your child there are different types of clouds that form in the sky. Teach them that clouds are large bunches of water drops or ice crystals up in the air.

3. See what shapes or pictures you can find in the clouds. Use language such as, "I see a dog with his tongue hanging out," or "That cloud looks like a scoop of ice cream!" Make sure to point to the cloud you are looking at.

4. Give your child time to look and think about what they are seeing. Ask them to describe what they find.

TIP *If there aren't many noticeable shapes, you can just observe the clouds. Are they moving fast or slowly? Do you see any other objects in the sky, such as birds or airplanes?*

Sound Search

This activity helps us slow down and notice the sounds in our environment. Simply get outside and listen. Even better, take a walk with a purpose!

Messiness: 1
Prep time: 5 minutes
Activity time:
5 to 15 minutes

MATERIALS

Printer and paper or notebook

Pencil or crayon

Clipboard (optional)

PREP

Print the Sound Search checklist (use the printable via the link in the Resources section on page 149), or create your own on a notebook page.

STEPS

1. Ask your toddler what part of their body they use to listen and hear sounds.

2. Tell them you are going to go on a hunt for sounds. Sit outside or go on a walk and listen carefully. Remind them that we can't hear well when others are talking, so it's important to stay quiet.

3. Once you've listened for a while, talk about what you heard. If you printed out the checklist, check off the sounds you heard!

Nature Soup

A bowl, a bucket of water, and whatever you can find around the yard become the most savory nature soup with a little imagination. You can even add some real spices to engage more senses.

Messiness: 3
Prep time: 5 minutes
Activity time: 15 minutes

MATERIALS

Large bowl or
plastic container

Pitcher of water

Spices, such as cumin,
oregano, pepper, and
paprika (optional)

Ladle or spoon

Smaller container
or bowls

Items from nature,
such as rocks, sticks,
bark, leaves, and
flower petals

PREP

Gather all the materials except for the
nature items.

STEPS

1. Tell your child it's time to get cooking! Your order is a big bowl of soup.

2. Have them pour some water from the pitcher into the large bowl.

3. Then walk around your yard or a park to find ingredients for the soup. Don't forget to talk about what each one could be. Are the rocks potatoes? Could the sticks be celery?

4. Add spices, if you choose.

5. Mix and stir. Keep adding ingredients until the soup's perfect!

6. Ladle the soup into smaller bowls to "serve." Maybe some toys would like to have a bowl, too?

CAUTION! *Take care not to pick items like small rocks that could be choking hazards. Be aware of any sticks with sharp points. Avoid picking berries. Some are poisonous!*

Bug Study

Find a little bug and give it a temporary home so you can observe it. Use a magnifying glass to be extra-scientific.

Messiness: 1
Prep time: None
Activity time: 10 minutes

MATERIALS

Clear plastic container with a lid (make sure to poke air holes in the lid if you plan to keep the bug for a while)

Items from nature, such as dirt, leaves, and sticks

Magnifying glass (optional)

STEPS

1. Prepare the container with your child to provide a nice little home for the insect. Spread a shallow layer of dirt in the bottom and some items from nature.

2. Go on a bug hunt.

3. Once you find your bug, gently place it in the container.

4. Observe and discuss! Does the bug ever stop moving? Does it eat anything? What colors is it? Do you think it likes the container, or would it rather be back in the wild?

5. Return your bug friend back to where you found it.

6. Look for another bug to observe, and repeat the activity.

Nature Patterns

Create fun patterns using things you find in nature. The options are endless!

Messiness: 1
Prep time: None
Activity time: 5 minutes

MATERIALS

Items from nature, such as rocks, leaves, flower petals, and sticks

Tray

Plain towel or mat (optional)

STEPS

1. Collect natural items with your child and lay them on a tray.

2. Create a simple ABAB pattern on your mat (or somewhere with a plain background, such as concrete). Say, "Here is a rock, a leaf, another rock, and another leaf. What do you think comes next?" Let your child continue making the pattern with the materials.

3. Use different materials for another ABAB pattern, such as: red flower, yellow flower, red flower, yellow flower.

4. If your child is ready for a new challenge, create an AAB pattern: rock, rock, stick, rock, rock, stick.

5. Try other patterns, such as AABB, AAAB, ABC, etc.

CAUTION! *Take care not to pick items like small rocks that could be choking hazards. Be aware of any sticks with sharp points. Avoid picking berries. Some are poisonous!*

Sprout a Seed

It's never too early to start learning where our food comes from. This activity will take a bit of patience to see results, but it is very exciting to watch the sprouts grow!

Messiness: 2
Prep time: None
Activity time: 5 minutes + observation time

MATERIALS

2 clear plastic cups

Seed-starting soil mix

Water

Spray bottle (optional)

Seeds, such as for herbs, fruits, vegetables, or flowers

Tape

STEPS

1. Fill one cup about three-quarters full with your soil mix. Add just enough water to make it damp. A spray bottle is helpful with this. Be careful not to overwater.

2. Plant your seed(s) using the directions on the seed packet.

3. Put the other cup upside down on top of the soil cup so the rims are touching.

4. Tape the rims together.

5. Place the cup in an area that will get full sun (outside is best). Moisture will appear on the inside of the cups.

6. Check back every day to see if your seeds have sprouted!

7. Once your seedlings sprout, you can remove the top cup. You will need to keep the soil damp.

8. Once the seedling has three or four leaves, you can transfer it to a pot or to your outdoor garden to watch it grow!

SKILLS
LEARNED

physics

gross motor
skills

following
directions

Animal Shadows

Has your child discovered their shadow yet? In this activity, your child will play a movement game to make different animal shadows with their body.

Messiness: 1
Prep time: **None**
Activity time: 5 minutes

MATERIALS

Just your bodies and a sunny day!

STEPS

1. Find a sunny space where you can easily see your shadow. Make sure your child can see their shadow in front of them on the ground.

2. Point out their shadow. Ask them to wave and see what the shadow does. Explain that shadows are made when an object blocks light.

3. Ask your child to squat down like a frog. Does their shadow look like a frog, too?

4. Have them stand up, hunch their back, and hold their arms out so they look like a bear. Does their shadow look like a bear, too?

5. Ask them to stand tall and reach their arms high above their head so they look like a giraffe. Does their shadow look like a giraffe, too?

6. Now play a movement game. Call out animal names and tell your child to position their body to match. Speed up your requests as your child gains confidence.

7. Invite your child to try making a different shadow animal with their body.

Nature Collection

Kids love to collect things. An egg carton is a great place to organize and display their nature treasures in a safe spot.

Messiness: 1
Prep time: 5 minutes
Activity time:
5 to 15 minutes

MATERIALS

Printer and paper

Scissors

Glue

Egg carton

Collection bag

PREP

1. Print the Nature Collection labels (use the printable via the link in the Resources section on page 149). Choose a type of collection. There are labels for rocks, flowers, leaves, colors, and nature in general.

2. Cut around the labels, and glue them to the inside of an egg carton lid. If your child is able to, you can have them cut out the labels and glue them in.

STEPS

1. Go on a nature hunt with your child for small objects that fit the category of their collection. Place your finds in the collection bag.

2. Organize your treasures by putting each item in its own compartment of the egg carton.

3. Your child can also slowly add to their collection when they find things of interest.

CAUTION! *Be sure you know what you are collecting. Some natural items are toxic or could cause an allergic reaction. Take care not to pick items like small rocks that could be choking hazards. Also, don't take things from private property without permission.*

Leaf Rubbings

This activity really helps little ones notice the details that make up a leaf. You can even make a memory game out of all your leaf rubbings!

Messiness: 2
Prep time: None
Activity time: 10 minutes

MATERIALS

Various leaves

White paper, cut into squares to fit your leaves (if you want to make a memory game, make them equal sizes)

Crayons

STEPS

1. Collect various leaves with your child.

2. Place a leaf beneath a paper square and rub a crayon over it. This works best if you remove the crayon wrapping and turn the crayon on its side. Ask your child to help after they watch you do it!

3. Pick a different color crayon and a new leaf and repeat.

4. Discuss the similarities and differences you see in the different leaves. What details do you notice?

TIP *If you want to make a memory game, make two rubbings of each type of leaf using the same crayon color.*

Nature Scavenger Hunt

Make your next hike a little more interesting with a nature scavenger hunt! This simple activity encourages observation, focus, and discussion about your surroundings. You can also go on a neighborhood scavenger hunt if there aren't parks or hiking areas nearby.

Messiness: 1
Prep time: 5 minutes
Activity time:
20 to 30 minutes

MATERIALS

Printer and paper or notebook

Pencil or crayon

Clipboard (optional)

PREP

Print out the Nature Scavenger Hunt checklist (use the printable via the link in the Resources section on page 149), or create your own on a notebook page.

STEPS

1. Go on a hike or a walk with your child and tell them to look for items on the list.

2. When your child spots an item, check its box on the list.

3. Count how many items they found!

fine motor skills	observation	botany	cause and effect	creativity	SKILLS LEARNED

Nature Stamps

Playdough is the perfect material for nature stamps. Your child can experiment with pressing leaves, sticks, flower petals, and rocks into it. Then roll the dough into a ball and start all over!

Messiness: 2
Prep time: 15 minutes
Activity time: 15 minutes

MATERIALS

Items from nature, such as leaves, rocks, petals, sticks, and bark

Playdough (recipe on page 60, or use store-bought)

Rolling pin (optional)

PREP

1. Gather nature items with your child.

2. Make your playdough, if you'd like.

STEPS

1. Ask your child to roll out the playdough with the rolling pin or push it down with their hands until the dough is flat.

2. Pick a nature object and show your child how to press it into the playdough.

3. Carefully remove the object and reveal the impression!

4. Let your child experiment with all the objects. When the dough Is covered in impressions, let your child squish it into a ball and roll it out again for a fresh canvas.

SKILLS
LEARNED   cause and   fine motor   gross motor   hand-eye
           effect   skills   skills   botany   coordination

Sticky Flower Wall

A sticky wall is perfect for toddlers because they are amazed by simply sticking things to it. This vertical activity works on toddlers' shoulder strength and hand-eye coordination.

Messiness: 2
Prep time: 5 minutes
Activity time: 10 minutes

MATERIALS

A variety of flowers, flower petals, or colorful leaves

Tray or towel

Contact paper

Scissors

Painter's tape

PREP

1. Arrange flowers on a tray or towel for your child to easily access.

2. Cut a piece of contact paper to make a large rectangle, about 2 feet wide.

3. Tape the contact paper to a wall at your child's height with the *sticky-side out.* It is helpful to peel a corner and tape it. Then continue to peel the backing and tape another corner. Repeat with the last two corners.

STEPS

1. Invite your child to choose a flower and stick it to the wall. Make a flower garden by sticking more!

2. Let them experiment. They can pick apart a flower and stick various pieces to the wall or stick the entire flower.

3. For a great autumn activity, stick colorful leaves on the wall instead!

botany	biology	language development	fine motor skills

Life Cycle Stones

Give your child something to paint other than paper! Make a set of painted rocks that illustrate a plant life cycle (seed, sprout, flower, fruit) or butterfly life cycle (egg, caterpillar, chrysalis, butterfly).

Messiness: 4
Prep time: 10 minutes
Activity time: 20 minutes

MATERIALS

Rocks (clean and flat)

Cardboard, news-paper, or paper towels

Acrylic paint, paint pens, or perma-nent markers, in various colors

Paper plate or paint palette (optional)

Paintbrush (optional)

PREP

1. Gather rocks from your yard or buy them from a craft store. Smooth stones without any type of finish work best. Rinse off any dirt and let them dry.

2. Cover the painting area with cardboard, news-paper, or paper towels.

3. Choose paint colors and squirt them on a paper plate or paint palette (if using).

STEPS

1. Invite your child to paint the rocks any color they'd like. Let the rocks dry.

2. Use paint, paint pens, or markers to paint or draw one step of the life cycle you choose on each rock. Let the rocks dry.

3. Talk to your toddler about each step in the life cycle as you put the rocks in a circle. Explain that the cycle repeats over and over again.

4. Pick up the rocks and ask your child to put them in order.

CAUTION! *Take care not to pick rocks that could be choking hazards. If it can fit through a toilet paper tube, find a bigger rock.*

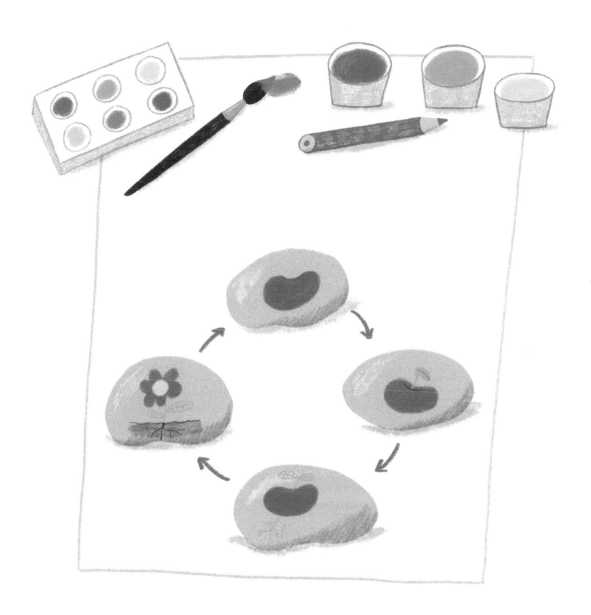

fine motor
skills

botany

cause and
effect

Making Juice

Squeezing fruit for juice is a great hand-strengthening activity to help those fine motor skills! Plus, it teaches your child where juice comes from and how it's made.

Messiness: 3
Prep time: 5 minutes
Activity time: 5 minutes

MATERIALS

Citrus fruit, such as lemons, limes, and oranges

Knife

Plate

Bowl

Cup

Strainer or spoon

PREP

Cut the fruit in half and then slice it into wedges. Set the fruit on a plate. Wash your hands and help your child wash theirs.

STEPS

1. Show your child how to squeeze the fruit wedge ends together to get the juice out. Do this over a bowl to collect the juice.

2. Have your toddler try to squeeze a wedge. Don't worry about the seeds at this point.

3. When your child has squeezed all the wedges, put the strainer over the cup and pour the juice from the bowl into the strainer to collect the seeds. If you don't have a strainer, you can scoop out the seeds from the bowl with a spoon.

4. Invite your child to take a little drink of the juice!

CAUTION! *Make sure the knife is not near your child when you are cutting the fruit.*

Watch a Plant Breathe

Do plants breathe? This activity will show your little scientist how leaves release oxygen—a gas we need to live.

Messiness: 2
Prep time: None
Activity time: 5 minutes + wait time

MATERIALS

Freshly picked leaf

Clear bowl

Water

Small rock

STEPS

1. Have your child fill the bowl up with room-temperature water.

2. Ask your child to examine the leaf. What does it feel like? Do you think it is breathing? Ask them what they think will happen when the leaf goes underwater.

3. Place the leaf under the rock in the bowl of water so it is fully submerged.

4. Put the bowl in sunlight and wait.

5. Check back after a few hours and look at the leaf. There should be tiny bubbles accumulating on the leaf and the edge of the bowl. This is the oxygen being released by the leaf.

CAUTION! *Take care not to pick rocks that could be choking hazards. If it can fit through a toilet paper tube, find a bigger rock.*

Trace the Parts of a Plant

Introduce your child to the parts of a plant while they also develop fine motor skills. Any chance to use a highlighter is exciting!

Messiness: 2
Prep time: 5 minutes
Activity time: 5 minutes

MATERIALS

Piece of white paper

Black marker

Highlighter

PREP

1. Using a black marker, draw a picture of a simple plant growing out of the ground. Illustrate the ground, roots, a stem, a leaf or two, and a flower on top.

2. If your child is ready to practice letters, you can label the parts of the flower, too.

STEPS

1. Invite your child to use the highlighter to draw along your black lines—starting with the ground and the roots.

2. As your child draws, talk about that part of the plant and what it does:

   • The roots hold the plant in the ground and suck up water and nutrients from the soil.

   • The stem carries water and nutrients to the leaves.

   • The leaves collect energy from the sun and make food for the plant.

   • The flower helps make new plants.

What's in the Grass?

Take a moment to settle in one spot on the grass and observe what's going on beneath your feet! Be still and watch. A magnifying glass is a great tool to help your little scientist look even closer.

Messiness: 1
Prep time: 5 minutes
Activity time: 5 minutes

MATERIALS

Hula-Hoop or string

Blanket (optional)

Magnifying glass (optional)

PREP

Choose an area in the grass for your child to focus on. Mark off the area with the Hula-Hoop or string. It shouldn't be any larger than the size of a Hula-Hoop. Lay a blanket down next to it if you'd like.

STEPS

1. Invite your child to look carefully at the ground. Ask them questions about what they see. What do they notice? What do the blades of grass look like? How do they feel? What's below the blades of grass? Do you see any creatures?

2. Stay put for a few minutes and see if anything changes.

- 3 -
MIX IT UP

These activities are all about mixing ingredients together and observing the changes. Some end results are fun to play with. Others you can eat!

We adults often think of these activities as prep work for play. But your toddler is actually your most eager helper. When you include them in the prep work, they learn a lot about science and math. They can help measure and stir. They learn to follow directions or a recipe and feel a sense of accomplishment with the end result.

Some of these mixtures result in messy play. Try to look beyond the mess and think about all the learning involved. You can make it easier on yourself by setting firm, clear boundaries. Talk about your expectations before the activity and be consistent with these boundaries. Also, make sure you stay close during the activity so you can monitor them and not let things get out of hand. If they do, remember to stay calm and simply stop the activity. It also helps to get messy outside or on days when the floor needs to be cleaned anyway!

SKILLS
LEARNED

measuring

following
directions

cause and
effect

gross motor
skills

language
development

Ice Cream in a Bag

Get ready to shake, shake, shake! Kids will get to watch their ingredients freeze through the process and enjoy a yummy treat in the end.

Messiness: 2
Prep time: None
Activity time: 20 minutes

MATERIALS

1 cup milk, or dairy-free alternative

2 tbsp sugar

1 tsp vanilla

Sandwich-size sealable plastic bag

4 cups ice

⅓ cup ice cream salt

Gallon-size sealable plastic bag

Toppings (optional)

STEPS

1. With your child's help, measure and pour the milk, sugar, and vanilla into the sandwich-size plastic bag. Seal well.

2. Put the ice, ice cream salt, and bag of liquid into the gallon-size plastic bag. Seal well.

3. Tell your toddler it's time to shake, shake, shake the bag until the liquid is frozen, about 10 minutes.

4. Put your now-frozen ice cream in a bowl, add any toppings (if using), and eat it up!

TIP *Things to do while shaking:*

- Ask how the bag feels. Is it cold, warm, soft, hard, wet, or dry?

- Observe how the bag's contents are changing from liquid to frozen.

- Sing some favorite songs and shake to the beat.

- Play a game and pass it back and forth like a hot potato.

| cause and effect | chemistry | observation | language development | following directions | SKILLS LEARNED |

Lava Lamp in a Cup

Not only is it fascinating to watch oil and water separate, but you will also get to see bubbles rise up that are reminiscent of the ones in lava lamps.

Messiness: 3
Prep time: None
Activity time: 10 minutes

MATERIALS

Clear glass or jar

Water

Food coloring

Spoon

Cooking oil

Effervescent antacid tablet

STEPS

1. Fill the glass about halfway with room-temperature water.

2. Add one or two drops of food coloring to your water. Have your toddler watch the color move through the water. Invite them to stir it with a spoon to mix.

3. Add the oil until it is about 1 inch from the top of your glass. Ask your toddler what they notice. Do the liquids mix together like the food coloring and water did?

4. Instruct your toddler to drop an antacid tablet into the glass and watch what happens!

TIP *You can use salt as an alternative, but the reaction won't be as big or last as long.*

CAUTION! *Make sure your child knows the materials in this activity are not for eating or drinking.*

Solid or Liquid?

Create a material that can be too hard to poke your finger in, but goopy enough to slide through your fingers. It is something you have to feel for yourself!

Messiness: 5
Prep time: None
Activity time: 20 minutes

MATERIALS

Large bowl or
9-by-12-inch
baking dish

2 cups cornstarch

Food coloring

1 cup water

Spoon

Small toy
figures (optional)

STEPS

1. Invite your child to pour the cornstarch into the bowl.

2. Add a few drops of food coloring to the water.

3. Pour about half of the water into the bowl of cornstarch. Ask your child to stir it with the spoon.

4. Add more water, if needed. It should be hard to stir toward the end, but when you pick up a chunk of the mixture, it will drip out of your hand. If you end up with too much water, you can always add more cornstarch to balance it out.

5. Have your child test it out! Can they poke their finger in it? Can they pick it up?

TIP *After your child has explored the texture, bury some toy figures in the goop and ask your child to find them.*

CAUTION! *Make sure your toddler knows this is not for eating.*

chemistry

sensory
development

measuring

following
directions

SKILLS
LEARNED

Toddler Slime

There are a lot of slime recipes out there, and most have ingredients that you may not want your toddler to handle. This recipe is safe for your toddler's skin, but it is not edible.

Messiness: 4
Prep time: None
Activity time: 20 minutes

MATERIALS

Large bowl

½ cup white glue

Food coloring

¼ cup shaving cream

1 tbsp baby lotion

1 tbsp baby oil

Spoon

3 tbsp Dreft liquid laundry detergent

STEPS

1. Pour the glue into the bowl.

2. Add a few drops of food coloring.

3. Add the shaving cream, baby lotion, and baby oil.

4. Invite your child to help stir it all together.

5. Add the laundry detergent, 1 tablespoon at a time, and stir in between. Once the slime sticks together in a blob, you know you have enough.

6. Show your toddler how to knead the mixture. It's ready when it stops sticking to your hands. If it is too sticky, add more laundry detergent.

7. Time to play! Encourage your child to stretch it, squish it, smash it, or poke it! What does it feel like if they step on it?

CAUTION! *Make sure your toddler knows this is not for eating.*

Fantastic Foam Fountain

Ready for a gushing surprise? This demonstration will have your little scientist in awe when the yeast and peroxide (plus a little dish soap) are combined.

Messiness: 5
Prep time: None
Activity time: 10 minutes

MATERIALS

½ cup hydrogen peroxide

Glass or jar

Dish soap

Food coloring

Small bowl

3 tbsp warm water

1 tbsp active dry yeast

Spoon

Large plastic bin or aluminum tray

STEPS

1. Pour the hydrogen peroxide into the glass.

2. Add a squirt of dish soap and swish it around to mix.

3. Add a few drops of food coloring, until the mixture is the color you'd like.

4. Put the warm water into the small bowl and add the yeast. Let your child mix it with a spoon to dissolve the yeast. It's okay if it still appears clumpy.

5. Put your glass of hydrogen peroxide mixture inside the large plastic bin or on the aluminum tray.

6. Have your toddler pour the yeast mixture into the glass and watch what happens!

CAUTION! *Make sure your toddler knows this is not for eating.*

Fizzy Fun

Do you know the classic volcano demonstration? Well, it doesn't have to be a volcano. You can observe this classic reaction on a much smaller scale. Your little scientist can even be in charge!

Messiness: **4**
Prep time: **None**
Activity time: **10 minutes**

MATERIALS

Pie pan or tray

Baking soda

Spoon

Vinegar

Cup

Medicine dropper or pipette

STEPS

1. Spoon little piles of baking soda onto your pie pan or tray.

2. Pour vinegar into the cup and instruct your child to use the medicine dropper or pipette to suck up some vinegar.

3. Have your child squeeze the vinegar over a baking soda pile and watch the fizzy reaction.

4. Move on to the next pile and see if the same thing happens!

5. Try adding water to one pile. Does the same reaction happen?

CAUTION! *Make sure your toddler knows this is not for eating.*

White Sand Beach

Also known as cloud dough, this mixture feels like soft, silky sand, but you can clump it together to form shapes. It's a wonderful sensory experience for toddlers!

Messiness: 5
Prep time: None
Activity time: 15 minutes

MATERIALS

Large bowl

4 cups flour

½ cup vegetable oil

Spoon

Plastic storage container or tray

Toys and tools, such as beach sand toys, sea-shells, animal figures, measuring spoons, and cups

STEPS

1. Ask your child to pour the flour into the bowl.

2. Add the oil.

3. Let your child help stir it with a spoon.

4. Once it's mixed, use your hands to squish the dough to make sure the ingredients are combined.

5. Pour the dough into a storage container. Now it's ready for sensory play! Add some toys and tools for your toddler to mold the dough with.

6. Store in an airtight container for later use.

CAUTION! *Flour can contain salmonella. You can microwave the dough before play for safety.*

Sensory Snow

This is a chilly science sensory activity! Snow is made of thousands of teeny-tiny ice crystals, but for this mixing experiment, you are going to use just two common household ingredients.

Messiness: 4

Prep time: None

Activity time: 15 minutes + 15 minutes freezing time

MATERIALS

Large bowl

¼ cup white hair conditioner

1 to 1½ cups baking soda, divided

Plastic storage container

Snow-themed toys

Spoon

STEPS

1. Ask your toddler to help you pour the conditioner and 1 cup of baking soda into a large bowl. Talk about how real snow is made of really tiny frozen water droplets, but today you are making pretend snow.

2. Let your child stir the ingredients together. Finish by kneading with your hands to make sure it's mixed well.

3. You now have snow that sticks together well for making snowmen and snowballs and is less messy. If you'd like more powdery snow (that still sticks together), add the remaining ½ cup of baking soda and stir.

4. Put your bowl in the freezer for about 15 minutes to make it nice and chilly. Set a timer so you don't forget about it.

5. Take your snow out of the freezer and put it into the storage container along with cookie cutters, toy cars, construction vehicles, toy snowplows, or polar animal figures for themed sensory play!

TIP *If you'd like more snow, double the batch!*

CAUTION! *Make sure your toddler knows this is not for eating.*

SKILLS
LEARNED   chemistry   sensory
development   measuring   following
directions

Jar of Fireworks

This is a really cool experiment to do on New Year's Eve or the Fourth of July. But this activity doesn't require your toddler to stay up way too late to get to participate in the fun!

Messiness: 2
Prep time: None
Activity time: 15 minutes

MATERIALS

Glass jar

Water

Small bowl

4 tbsp cooking oil

Food coloring

Spoon

STEPS

1. Fill the glass jar three-quarters of the way full with water.

2. Pour the cooking oil into the small bowl.

3. Have your child stir a few drops of food coloring into the oil as you drop them in. The food coloring will only break down into smaller drops. Don't expect the liquids to mix together.

4. Pour the oil into the jar of water.

5. Observe what happens! Spoiler alert: The oil will settle on top of the water, but the food coloring drops will sink down and hit the water in a beautiful display.

CAUTION! *Make sure your toddler knows this is not for drinking.*

Salty Watercolors

Painting with glue and salt is fun for all ages! This is a science activity that also serves as a process-focused art project. Let your child take the lead and see where they take it.

Messiness: **4**
Prep time: **None**
Activity time: **15 minutes**

MATERIALS

Card stock, cardboard, foam board, or canvas (paper is too flimsy)

Bottle of white glue

Tray with tall sides or rimmed baking sheet

Salt

Liquid watercolors or watered-down food coloring, in various colors

Paintbrush

STEPS

1. Have your child squeeze lines of glue on the card stock. You can help them draw a picture (rainbow lines, hearts, snowflakes, fireworks, etc.) or write a number or letter, or let them make their own designs.

2. Place the card stock in the tray and have your child sprinkle the salt so it covers all the glue.

3. Lift up the card stock so the excess salt falls back in the tray.

4. Instruct your child to dip their paintbrush in the watercolor and gently touch it to the salt-covered glue. Watch it spread!

5. Continue until all the lines are colored.

6. Let it dry thoroughly—it may take overnight.

TIP *If your toddler isn't so gentle and smears the glue and salt all over, that's okay! It's process art, and that's their process.*

CAUTION! *Make sure your toddler knows this is not for eating.*

Homemade Whipped Cream

Making your own whipped cream is easy, fun, and delicious! It's also a neat science activity for your toddler, because the cream changes from liquid to fluffy right before their eyes.

Messiness: **2**
Prep time: **None**
Activity time: **10 minutes**

MATERIALS

Large mixing bowl

1 pint heavy (whipping) cream

1 tsp vanilla extract

1 tbsp powdered sugar (you can leave this out if you want a "no added sugar" option)

Hand mixer or stand mixer

STEPS

1. Ask your toddler to pour the whipping cream into the mixing bowl.

2. Add the vanilla and powdered sugar.

3. Set the mixer to the medium-high setting and beat the cream until it forms soft peaks. It will take a few minutes. Don't be afraid to stop mixing to test the consistency. If you mix it too much, it will become solid and turn to butter. (That's another experiment in itself!)

4. Time to enjoy the whipped cream! Dip fresh fruit in it, add it to hot cocoa, or make an ice cream sundae bar. Yum!

TIP *If you're using a stand mixer, use the wire whisk attachment and don't walk away! The cream can thicken suddenly.*

CAUTION! *Make sure your toddler knows to never put their hands near the mixer.*

Make Guacamole—Olé!

Guacamole is one of my kids' favorite things to help with in the kitchen. It's a big deal for a toddler to be in control and mash those avocados up. This is how I've been making it since my mom taught me!

Messiness: 3
Prep time: None
Activity time: 10 minutes

MATERIALS

2 ripe avocados

Knife

Large bowl

Spoon

Potato masher

¼ cup salsa, plus more to taste

Garlic salt

Black pepper

STEPS

1. Cut the avocados in half and remove the pits. Cut the flesh of each half (but not through the skin) vertically and horizontally so you get diced chunks. As you work, talk about knife safety with your toddler.

2. Have your toddler help scoop the avocado into the bowl with the spoon.

3. Show your child how to use the potato masher to smash the avocado. Hand it over to them while you hold the bowl in place.

4. Mash until the avocado is the consistency you want.

5. Add the salsa.

6. Add garlic salt and pepper to taste.

7. Have your child stir it all together.

8. Taste test! Get a chip or a vegetable for you and your child and sample the guacamole. Add more salsa, garlic salt, or pepper, if desired.

CAUTION! *Make sure the sharp knife is not near your child when you are cutting the avocados.*

Jumping Raisins

This activity takes just two items from your pantry and is a really fun and simple science demonstration.

Messiness: 1
Prep time: **None**
Activity time: **5 minutes**

MATERIALS

Clear glass or jar

Seltzer or clear soda

Small handful of raisins

STEPS

1. Ask your child to pour the seltzer into the glass until it's about halfway full.

2. Have your child add several raisins to the glass.

3. Observe what happens! The raisins will sink to the bottom, but if you wait, they will float to the top. If you wait some more, they will return to the bottom.

TIP *You can also use popcorn kernels or dried beans instead of raisins.*

Frothy Foam Fun

Make a bath time sensory bin—outside the bathtub! Just mix dish soap and water and use a mixer to froth it up and make loads of foam.

Messiness: **4**
Prep time: **None**
Activity time: **20 minutes**

MATERIALS

Large bowl

½ cup water

¼ cup dish soap or toddler-safe liquid soap

Hand mixer or blender

Storage tub

Play objects, such as teacups, measuring cups, spoons, and whisks

STEPS

1. Have your child pour the water into the bowl.

2. Instruct them to add the soap.

3. Have your toddler watch the foam grow as you beat the soap and water with a hand mixer on the highest speed.

4. Transfer the foam into an empty tub for sensory play. Provide a few objects to encourage imaginative play.

TIP *If your child is very young and may touch their eyes and face, use baby shampoo so the foam won't sting.*

CAUTION! *Make sure your toddler knows this is not for eating and that they should never put their hands near the mixer.*

SKILLS
LEARNED   chemistry   sensory
                           development   measuring   following
                                                       directions

DIY Playdough

This is an easy recipe that you don't have to cook. Just add the ingredients and mix! Make it your own by adding essential oils or spices for a subtle scent.

Messiness: **4**
Prep time: **None**
Activity time: **20 minutes**

MATERIALS

2½ cups hot water

Large bowl

4 cups flour

3 tbsp cream of tartar

1 cup salt

¼ cup vegetable oil

Spoon

Food coloring

Essential oils (peppermint, lavender, etc.) (optional)

Hand mixer or stand mixer

STEPS

1. Boil water on the stove or in the microwave.

2. Place the flour in the large bowl.

3. Ask your child to help add the cream of tartar, salt, and vegetable oil.

4. Have your toddler stir it until everything is mixed well.

5. Stir a few drops of food coloring into the water. Add a few drops of essential oils, if desired.

6. Slowly pour the hot water into the bowl of dry ingredients.

7. Mix with a hand mixer or use a dough hook in a stand mixer.

8. Make sure the dough is not too hot. Then knead the dough until it's thoroughly blended. Your child can help, too, if the dough is cool enough!

9. Time to play!

CAUTION! *Make sure your toddler knows this is not for eating. This activity requires boiling water and a mixer. Talk with your toddler about those dangers and keep them safely away.*

chemistry

sensory
development

measuring

following
directions

SKILLS
LEARNED

Bubble Play

Making your own bubble solution is easy, and this recipe makes a large container of it for hours of fun. You can even experiment with your own bubble wands!

Messiness: **4**
Prep time: **None**
Activity time: **20 minutes**

MATERIALS

Shoebox-size storage
bin with a lid

6 cups warm water
(distilled water is
best, but tap water
will work)

1 cup liquid dish soap

Spoon

¼ cup light corn syrup

Bubble wand or
pipe cleaner

STEPS

1. Have your child pour the water into the bin.

2. Let them add the dish soap.

3. Stir slowly, trying not to let bubbles or foam form.

4. Add in the corn syrup and mix slowly.

5. You can use the solution right away, but if you put the lid on and let it sit overnight, you will have extra-good bubbles.

6. Use a bubble wand from an old jar of bubbles or make your own out of a pipe cleaner. Twist one end of the pipe cleaner into a circle to form a wand.

CAUTION! *Make sure your toddler knows this is not for eating.*

Sensory Bottle

Calming sensory bottles are great to have when your little one is experiencing big feelings. Now your budding scientist can help you make one!

Messiness: 2
Prep time: **None**
Activity time: 15 minutes

MATERIALS

Plastic bottle

Water

Food coloring

Glitter, beads, or sequins (optional)

Baby oil

Hot glue

Hot glue gun

STEPS

1. Pour water into the plastic bottle until it's two-thirds full.

2. Add a drop or two of food coloring.

3. Drop in any small items you choose, such as glitter, beads, or sequins (if using).

4. Add the oil until it is near the top of the bottle.

5. Secure the lid with hot glue so your child can't unscrew it. Do this away from your child, since it is extremely hot. Let it dry.

6. Turn over the bottle and watch the bubbles and swirls! Point out to your child that the oil and water don't mix, and they never will.

7. Put the bottle down and watch it settle.

CAUTION! *Hot glue guns are extremely hot. Make sure it is plugged in in an area that your child cannot reach and will not be nearby. The items you drop in may be choking hazards.*

SKILLS
LEARNED

chemistry

sensory
development

creativity

following
directions

Bath Paint

Make bath time extra-fun with this safe, easy paint that gets rinsed down the drain when it's time to clean up!

Messiness: 5
Prep time: None
Activity time: 20 minutes

MATERIALS

Large bowl

½ cup cornstarch

1 cup baby shampoo

Spoon

Muffin pan

Food coloring, in various colors

Paintbrushes (optional)

STEPS

1. Put the cornstarch and baby shampoo in the bowl.

2. Ask your child to mix them together with the spoon.

3. Spoon the mixture into the cups of a muffin pan.

4. Add a different drop of food coloring to each cup and stir to blend. I've used up to five drops and the paint didn't stain my child's skin or the tub.

5. Take your muffin pan to the bath or shower and get painting with fingers or paintbrushes (if using)!

6. When it's time to clean up, simply use water to rinse your toddler's creations off the walls and down the drain. If the paint dries, you'll need just a little scrubbing power with your hand or a cloth.

CAUTION! *Make sure your toddler knows this is not for eating. Paint may also make the tub slippery.*

Disappearing Lollipop

Put a lollipop upside down in water and it will slowly disappear. This is a great visual to teach children the concept of dissolving.

Messiness: 1
Prep time: None
Activity time: 5 minutes + observation time

MATERIALS

Clear cup or jar

Water

Lollipop

STEPS

1. Fill the cup with enough water so the lollipop will be covered.

2. Have your child put the lollipop in the water upside down. Ask your child what they think will happen to the lollipop.

3. While it will take about an hour for the candy to dissolve completely, you will start to see the water change color after a few minutes. Your child can pull out the stick periodically to check the lollipop's status.

4. If you don't mind the sugar, you can let your child taste the lollipop water.

Melted Chocolate

Watch chocolate chips change shape as they are heated up. Then make the most of it by dipping strawberries in the melted chocolate to eat!

Messiness: 2
Prep time: 5 minutes
Activity time: 10 minutes

MATERIALS

Strawberries

Microwave-safe bowl

1 cup semisweet chocolate chips

Spoon

Wax paper

PREP

Wash your strawberries and let them dry.

STEPS

1. Have your toddler measure and pour the chocolate chips into a microwave-safe bowl.

2. Microwave the chips for about 30 seconds.

3. Take out the bowl. You should see some chips partially melted, but others not.

4. If the bowl isn't too hot, have your child stir the chocolate chips. They should begin to melt together.

5. Microwave the chips for 30 more seconds. Stir again. If the chips still aren't completely melted, microwave for 10-second increments until they are.

6. Lay out a piece of wax paper.

7. Have your child dip a strawberry in the melted chocolate. Then lay it on the wax paper to harden. Repeat for the rest of the strawberries.

8. Have a taste and talk about how the chocolate chips were hard at first, then they were melted with heat, and once they cooled, they hardened up again!

9. Refrigerate any leftovers.

CAUTION! *The chocolate and dish may be hot.*

Puffy Paint

This paint is especially fun because it's puffy after it dries!

Messiness: 3
Prep time: 5 minutes
Activity time: 15 minutes

MATERIALS

Card stock
or cardboard

Marker

Large bowl

½ cup white glue

½ cup shaving cream

Spoon

Small bowls or muffin
pan (optional)

Food coloring or liquid
watercolors, in various
colors (optional)

Paintbrush

PREP

Use a marker to draw an outline of what your child will be painting on the card stock or cardboard. They will paint inside the lines. An easy first project is cloud outlines on blue card stock.

STEPS

1. Place the glue and shaving cream in the large bowl.

2. Have your child thoroughly stir to mix.

3. If you want to make different colors, separate the mixture into small bowls or a muffin pan and add a few drops of food coloring or liquid watercolor. Stir to mix.

4. Instruct your little artist to paint inside the lines. The more paint, the better! You want it to be thick, because the paint flattens a bit as it dries.

5. Let the painting dry overnight.

TIP *Paint scoops of ice cream and use tan paper triangles for the cones. Try painting a snowman. While the paint is still wet, drop in black beans for eyes and a paper carrot nose!*

CAUTION! *Make sure your toddler knows this is not for eating.*

- 4 -
TOUCH AND FEEL

Young children use their sense of touch as a way to explore and learn about their environments. The activities in this chapter involve feeling various objects and textures.

Not all children enjoy this process, and that's okay. Some kids love a good mess. Others prefer not to get their hands dirty. You can meet your child where they are. If your child enjoys these types of sensory experiences, encourage them to dive in and explore. If your child is more hesitant, let them do what it takes to feel comfortable. Perhaps they can use a spoon as an extension of their hand so they can experiment without getting messy. Keep offering sensory activities for them, because one day they may decide to go for it!

SKILLS
LEARNED

sensory
development

fine motor
skills

cause and
effect

creativity

Taste-Safe Finger Painting

Finger painting is a childhood delight! Do you ever worry those colorful fingers are going to end up in your child's mouth? This activity is taste-safe, just in case that happens.

Messiness: 5
Prep time: 5 minutes
Activity time: 15 minutes

MATERIALS

Plain yogurt (large tub or several small containers)

Food coloring, in various colors

Paper plate (optional)

A canvas, such as a highchair tray, finger paint paper, or the bathtub

PREP

1. Mix some yogurt with a drop or two of food coloring. This small amount won't stain fingers, but it may if you use several more drops. Repeat for each color.

2. Arrange the colors on a "plate palette" or keep them in individual containers.

STEPS

1. Put the child in front of their canvas. If you'd like easy cleanup, let them paint the walls next to the bathtub and wash it down the drain. You can also do the activity outside with paper.

2. Introduce the activity to the child. Make sure to let them know paint is for painting with, not for eating.

3. Let your child create and explore!

SKILLS
LEARNED

physics

observation

language
development

Explore a Spoon

Usually we think of sensory items as soft, squishy things, but for this activity we are going to take a deeper look at a hard, shiny object—a spoon!

Messiness: 1
Prep time: None
Activity time: 5 minutes

MATERIALS

Metal spoon

STEPS

1. Give your toddler a metal spoon. Ask them how it feels. Is it hard or soft? Light or heavy?

2. Instruct them to look up close at the scoop part of the spoon (the concave side). What do they see? The reflection of their face on the spoon will be upside down.

3. Turn the spoon over to the convex side (the side that's rounded out) and tell your child to look closely. How is their reflection different? Their face will be right-side up!

Squishy Bag

There are so many versions of this simple activity that will thoroughly enthrall even the littlest ones! You just need a clear bag, water, tape, and pretty much any small object you'd like to put inside.

Messiness: 1
Prep time: None
Activity time: 5 minutes

MATERIALS

Gallon-size sealable bag (a reusable silicone bag is best)

Water

Small objects, such as pom-poms, flowers, googly eyes, sequins, pony beads, peas, and water beads

Painter's tape

STEPS

1. Fill the bag up with water and add the pom-poms or any other small object you'd like.

2. Seal up the bag and tape down each side to your counter or your floor.

3. Invite your child to explore the bag. Let them touch, poke, squish, etc. Ask them how it feels. How many objects can they count? What colors are the objects?

CAUTION! *The items you drop in may be choking hazards.*

Pipe Cleaner Shapes

Create sensory shape cards that your toddler can trace with their fingers. This is a fun tactile way to explore shapes!

Messiness: 1
Prep time: 10 minutes
Activity time: 5 minutes

MATERIALS

Cardboard

Scissors

Pipe cleaners

Hot glue

Hot glue gun

PREP

1. Cut the cardboard into 4-inch squares.

2. Bend the pipe cleaners into different shapes: circle, square, triangle, rectangle, etc.

3. Use the hot glue gun to secure one shape on to each piece of cardboard. Do this away from your child, since it is extremely hot. Let it dry.

STEPS

1. Invite your child to take their finger and trace it along the pipe cleaner.

2. Name the shape as they are tracing it. Say, "That is a square."

3. Count the sides as they trace. Say, "It has one, two, three, four sides that are all the same length."

CAUTION! *Hot glue guns are extremely hot. Make sure it is plugged in in an area that your child cannot reach and will not be nearby.*

sensory
development

fine motor
skills

SKILLS
LEARNED

Shaving Cream in the Tub

As a teacher, I would squirt shaving cream on each child's desk to let them play *and* get it clean for Open House. Now I squirt it in the tub for my kids to play, write, and draw—while also cleaning the tub!

Messiness: 4
Prep time: None
Activity time: 20 minutes

MATERIALS

Shaving cream

Tub or shower

STEPS

1. Squirt a good amount of shaving cream in the tub.

2. Have your child sit in the tub and spread out the shaving cream with their hands.

3. Invite them to use their fingers to draw pictures or different types of lines.

4. They can use their hands to erase and create a new canvas once again.

CAUTION! *This activity can be very slippery. Don't allow kids to stand while they are playing. Adult supervision required.*

Hard vs. Soft

Classifying objects is a big skill for little ones to learn. For this activity, they will be feeling groups of items and deciding which one object does not belong.

Messiness: 1
Prep time: None
Activity time: 5 minutes

MATERIALS

Hard items, such as board books, blocks, rocks, cups, and plates

Soft items, such as pillows, stuffed animals, cotton balls, feathers, and flowers

STEPS

1. Ask your child to handle each of the hard items. What does your child hear when they hit the object on the ground or against another item? What happens when they squeeze the object? Explain that these are all hard objects. Hard objects make noise when they're hit against something, and you can't squish them by squeezing.

2. Now ask your child to handle each of the soft items. What does your child hear when they hit the object on the ground? What happens when they squeeze the object? Explain that these are all soft objects. Soft objects don't make much noise, and they do squish when you squeeze them.

3. Mix all the items into one big pile.

4. Tell your child you are going to play a game of "What doesn't belong?" Pick four objects out of the big pile: three hard and one soft.

5. Ask your child to point to which one is different. Can they tell you why it's different?

6. Repeat with a new set of four objects.

sensory
development

language
development

following
directions

SKILLS
LEARNED

Guess the Object

This activity relies completely on the sense of touch. Your child will reach into a bag and guess what the object inside is by feeling it.

Messiness: 1
Prep time: None
Activity time: 5 minutes

MATERIALS

Small paper bag

Small textured objects, such as oranges, rocks, feathers, leaves, flowers, toys, blocks, and crayons

Scarf or blindfold (optional)

STEPS

1. Put one of the items in the paper bag.

2. Wrap a scarf or blindfold around your child's eyes if you think they might peek.

3. Tell your child to reach into the bag and feel the object. Encourage them to imagine what it could be.

4. Ask them to make a guess before they pull it out.

5. Repeat for another object.

| physics | sensory development | fine motor skills | creativity | problem-solving | shapes |

Pretzel Structures

Sometimes it's okay to play with your food! This activity encourages kids to build with pretzels and marshmallows.

Messiness: 2
Prep time: 5 minutes
Activity time: 20 minutes

MATERIALS

Pretzel sticks

Marshmallows

2 plates or a tray

PREP

Arrange the marshmallows and pretzel sticks on two different plates or a tray.

STEPS

1. Show your child how to push the end of a pretzel stick into the bottom of a marshmallow.

2. Invite them to try it on their own.

3. Ask your child to connect two sticks with a marshmallow.

4. Encourage them to build a shape, design, or letter with their pretzels and marshmallows. Feel free to eat what you build!

TIP *Fun shapes to try are letters or a snowflake. Your child can also try a three-dimensional shape, like a box or house!*

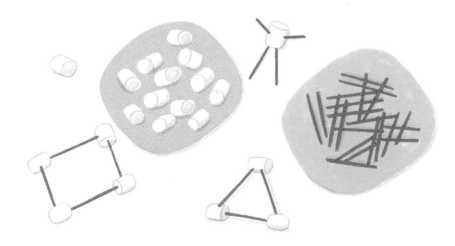

Seeing Seeds

Make some time for a little seed exploration while you are prepping for a meal.

Messiness: 3
Prep time: 5 minutes
Activity time: 10 minutes

MATERIALS

Several fruits, such as stone fruit, strawberry, orange, grape, banana, kiwi, and avocado

Knife

PREP

Wash your fruit.

STEPS

1. Teach your toddler that for something to be called a fruit, it must have seeds!

2. Hold up a stone fruit and ask your child if they see any seeds.

3. Cut around the pit of the stone fruit and ask your child if they see any seeds. It's in the middle of the fruit! Set the pit aside to explore later.

4. Hold up a strawberry and ask your child to look for seeds. Point out all the tiny seeds on the strawberry's skin.

5. Start to peel an orange and let your child help you. Ask your child if they can find the seeds.

6. Repeat with other fruits. You can even see tiny seeds in the middle of a banana or grape!

7. Let your child touch all the food scraps and seeds you saved while you finish making fruit salad!

CAUTION! *Make sure the sharp knife is not near your child when you are cutting the fruit. Supervise your child while they are exploring. Some larger seeds can be choking hazards.*

SKILLS
LEARNED

language
development

sensory
development

fine motor
skills

Touch the Textures

From rough sandpaper to soft fur, let your child explore textures in a non-messy way! This texture board is simple to make and easy to store for an activity to enjoy again and again.

Messiness: 1
Prep time: 10 minutes
Activity time: 20 minutes

MATERIALS

Large piece of card-
board or poster board

Items that vary in
texture, such as a
sponge, leather, silk,
flannel, lace, contact
paper, sandpaper,
and yarn

Hot glue

Hot glue gun

Painter's tape
(optional)

PREP

Use hot glue to secure your textures (about a 4-by-4-inch square of each) to the cardboard in rows. Do this away from your child, since it is extremely hot. Let it dry.

STEPS

1. Set your board vertically against a wall (use painter's tape to secure it, if desired) or lay it flat on the ground.

2. Explain to your child that the sense of touch is one of our five senses and we can feel things on our skin.

3. Invite your child to touch the different textures.

4. Have your child describe what they are feeling. For example: "That sandpaper is very rough." "This fur is soft." "The contact paper is sticky!"

CAUTION! *Hot glue guns are extremely hot. Make sure it is plugged in in an area that your child cannot reach and will not be nearby. Make sure all items are large enough to not be choking hazards in case they come loose from the board.*

sensory
development

physics

fine motor
skills

SKILLS
LEARNED

Gelatin Dig

Make gelatin and throw in some of your child's toy figures before you put it in the refrigerator. Once the gelatin is set, you will have a delightful sensory experience for your toddler.

Messiness: 5
Prep time: 5 minutes +
1 hour 30 minutes
to set
Activity time: 10 minutes

MATERIALS

Box of gelatin

Deep baking dish

Toy figures

Large tray or plastic shower curtain

Bowl of warm water

Spoon

Tweezers or tongs (optional)

PREP

Prepare the gelatin according to the package directions and pour the mixture into a deep baking dish. Add some toy figures to the dish. Refrigerate until set.

STEPS

1. Lay out the large tray or shower curtain for easy cleanup.

2. Set the dish of gelatin on it, along with the bowl of warm water and spoon.

3. Invite your child to dig out the toys! They can use the spoon, or try tweezers or tongs (if using) for fine motor skill practice. They can also explore with their hands (although it may stain skin).

4. Rinse the toys in the warm water and let them dry.

SKILLS
LEARNED   sensory
development   colors   fine motor
skills   language
development   creativity

Mess-Free Painting

When you aren't feeling up to a mess-making activity, opt for painting in a bag!

Messiness: 1
Prep time: 5 minutes
Activity time: 10 minutes

MATERIALS

Poster board or white card stock

Scissors

Gallon-size sealable bag

Tempera or finger paint, in various colors

PREP

1. Cut the poster board or card stock to fit in the plastic bag.

2. Place a small amount (about 1 tablespoon) of each color of paint in various spots on the poster board or card stock. Use red, yellow, and blue if you want to experiment with making new colors!

3. Slide the paper inside the bag and seal well.

STEPS

1. Invite your child to use their fingers or hands to move the paint around. Do they see any new colors?

2. Ask them how the paint feels through the bag. Is it squishy or hard?

3. Ask your child to draw lines and shapes or letters and numbers.

4. If you'd like to keep their artwork, remove it from the bag and let it dry.

Floating Fruits

Take water play up a notch by adding sliced fruit. Your little scientist can check to see if the pieces sink or float and explore another sensory experience—smell!

Messiness: 4
Prep time: 5 minutes
Activity time: 20 minutes

MATERIALS

Fruit, such as lemons, oranges, limes, cucumbers, and kiwis

Knife

Large storage tub or water table

Tarp or shower curtain (optional)

Water

Kitchen items, such as ladles, bowls, spoons, and whisks

PREP

Slice the fruit into circular discs, leaving the peels on.

STEPS

1. Take the storage tub outside. Alternatively, lay down a tarp or shower curtain on the floor indoors.

2. Fill the tub with water. Your toddler can help by pouring pitchers of water into the tub.

3. Add the sliced fruit to the water.

4. Ask your toddler if the fruit sinks or floats.

5. Invite your child to touch the fruits and describe how the fruits feel. If you used different fruits, ask how they look different. It's okay if your child wants to take off the peels or take out the seeds, etc.

6. Give your child the kitchen items and let them play. Encourage them to transfer the fruit to a bowl.

CAUTION! *Make sure the sharp knife is not near your child when you are cutting the fruit. Also make sure your child knows not to eat the seeds or peels of the fruit. Never leave your child unattended by water.*

physics	sensory development	fine motor skills	hand-eye coordination

Thread the Os

This activity combines the squishy texture of playdough with the hard, crunchy texture of cereal. It is a simple and fun way to build fine motor skills and hand-eye coordination!

Messiness: 2
Prep time: None
Activity time: 10 minutes

MATERIALS

Playdough (recipe on page 60, or use store-bought)

Dry spaghetti noodles

Any cereal with a hole in the center

STEPS

1. Have your child shape the playdough into a ball or mound and set it on a flat surface.

2. Instruct them to stick the spaghetti noodles into the playdough, so the noodles stand up vertically. Break the noodles in half if they are too long.

3. Ask your child to thread the cereal Os onto the spaghetti.

TIP *If the spaghetti noodles are too fragile and break easily, you can use wooden dowels and dry rigatoni pasta instead.*

CAUTION! *Make sure your child knows this is not for eating. The dried noodles could be sharp.*

Sensory Spaghetti

Next time you make spaghetti for dinner, cook a little extra for this very simple sensory bin. The squirmy, squishy bucket of noodles will delight your toddler.

Messiness: 3

Prep time: 15 minutes + cooling time

Activity time: 10 minutes

MATERIALS

Uncooked spaghetti noodles

Large tray or baking dish

Cooking oil (optional)

Bowl

Tongs (optional)

PREP

1. Prepare the spaghetti according to the package directions.

2. Strain and let cool.

STEPS

1. Put the cooked and cooled spaghetti noodles in a large tray or baking dish. Add a little oil if the noodles are sticky.

2. Invite your child to handle the noodles. Ask your child how the noodles feel.

3. Set an empty bowl nearby. Encourage them to transfer the noodles to the bowl. Tongs are another fun way to do this.

TIP *You can hide small toys or food items in the noodles for your toddler to find. If you have an older toddler, cutting the spaghetti noodles is also a great way to practice proper scissor skills.*

CAUTION! *If you added oil, the noodles could stain clothing or furniture.*

SKILLS
LEARNED

physics

sensory
development

fine motor
skills

measuring

hand-eye
coordination

Rice Filling Station

A bucket of rice has a fascinating texture, even for grown-ups! In this activity, your toddler will learn about volume and gravity while also working on scooping and transferring skills.

Messiness: 3
Prep time: None
Activity time: 20 minutes

MATERIALS

Large sheet or towel

Large storage bucket

1 (5- or 10-pound) bag uncooked rice

Kitchen items, such as measuring cups, bowls, spoons, muffin pans, and strainers

STEPS

1. Lay out the sheet or towel on the ground. This will make it very easy to collect any rice that misses the bucket.

2. Set your storage bucket on the towel and dump in the bag of rice and kitchen items.

3. Invite your child to fill up the cups, dump them out, and transfer from one container to another.

4. Ask them questions like, "How many of these scoops does it take to fill this bowl?" or "Why do you think the rice always falls down when you pour it out?"

CAUTION! *Make sure your child knows this rice isn't for eating.*

What's in the Balloon?

Fill balloons with various materials to let your toddler squeeze and explore. Can they guess what's inside?

Messiness: 3
Prep time: None
Activity time: 10 minutes

MATERIALS

Balloons

Funnel

Flour

Dry rice

Beans

Water

Shampoo

Popcorn kernels

STEPS

1. Blow up a balloon to stretch it out a bit, but then let the air out.

2. Slip the end of the balloon around the funnel and ask your toddler to help fill the balloon about halfway full with flour.

3. Tie a knot in the balloon.

4. Repeat, using other sensory items in the materials list. The beans may not fit through the funnel, so you can put them in by hand—a great job for your toddler!

5. Hand the balloons over to your child for them to touch and squeeze. Ask them if they can guess which item is in each balloon.

CAUTION! *Balloon parts and some items can be choking hazards.*

SKILLS
LEARNED

physics

cause and effect

comparing

language development

Which Is Heavier?

This homemade scale is a great tool to get little ones to understand weight and compare objects.

Messiness: 1
Prep time: 5 minutes
Activity time: 10 minutes

MATERIALS

Hole puncher

2 paper cups

2 (18-inch) pieces of string or yarn

Hanger with notches

Objects to weigh, such as toy figures, plastic blocks, oranges, and crayons

PREP

1. Punch two holes directly across from each other in both cups, about ½ inch from the top.

2. Put one end of the string through a hole and tie it. Repeat with the other hole.

3. Do the same with the other string and cup.

STEPS

1. Put the hanger somewhere where your child can reach, like a doorknob or cupboard handle.

2. Hang one cup in the notch on each end of the hanger. The cups should be balanced.

3. Ask your child to pick two objects and place one in each cup. What happens?

4. Explain that the object in the cup that moved down was heavier, while the object in the cup that went up was lighter.

5. Repeat with different pairs of objects.

CAUTION! *Make sure your child doesn't put the cup with the string attached around their neck. That could be a strangulation hazard.*

SKILLS
LEARNED

physics

cause and
effect

sensory
development

imagination

Stale Stuff Sensory Bin

Use up stale pantry items by letting your toddler crush them up in a bag. Then add the items to a sensory bin to make an interesting construction site.

Messiness: 3
Prep time: None
Activity time: 20 minutes

MATERIALS

Stale pantry items, such as cereal, crackers, and cookies

Large sealable bag

Unbreakable cup

Storage bin

Toys and objects, such as construction vehicles, cones, mini shovels, mini figures, rocks, and sticks

STEPS

1. Pour the pantry items into the bag and seal it up.

2. Hand your toddler the cup and show them how to crush the contents by pressing the bottom of the cup into them.

3. When the contents are crushed, pour them into the storage bin.

4. Invite your toddler to feel the mixture, and ask them how it feels. Is it rough or smooth? Hard or soft? Heavy or light?

5. Add the toys and objects and watch your child's imagination get to work.

CAUTION! *Make sure nothing you add to the bin is a choking hazard.*

Straw Blowing

In this activity, your child will get to see if they have the lung power to make things move!

Messiness: 1
Prep time: None
Activity time: 10 minutes

MATERIALS

Heavy items, such as rocks, oranges, toy figures, books, and spoons

Light items, such as feathers, sprinkles, shredded paper, grass clippings, and leaves

Drinking straw

STEPS

1. Ask your child to help gather light and heavy objects from around the house. Put them in a line on the floor or counter.

2. Show your child how to blow through the straw. Have your child put their hand in front of the straw to feel the air pass through.

3. Ask them to aim the straw at an object and blow.

4. Talk about what happened. Did the object move? Did it fall over? If your child continues to blow, does it move farther?

5. Repeat with the next object.

6. Explain how the lighter objects can be easily moved with air, while the heavier objects don't move much, if at all.

CAUTION! *Take care when using the straw so it doesn't poke anyone or the roof of your child's mouth. Also, don't pick rocks that could be choking hazards. If it can fit through a toilet paper tube, find a bigger rock.*

Static Cling

Create static electricity with the help of your little scientist and a balloon.

Messiness: 1
Prep time: None
Activity time: 5 minutes

MATERIALS

Balloon

Wall

Head of hair or wool fabric

STEPS

1. Blow up the balloon and tie it.

2. Hold the balloon against a wall and let go. Ask your child what happened to the balloon.

3. Ask your child if you can rub the balloon on their hair. If they don't like it, rub it on your own hair to create a static charge. Alternatively, you can rub the balloon on a piece of wool fabric.

4. Hold the balloon against the wall again and let go. Ask your child what's happening now. If the balloon starts to fall, you can recharge it by rubbing it on your head again.

CAUTION! *Balloon parts can be choking hazards. Also, do not do this activity around electrical appliances or if you have a pacemaker.*

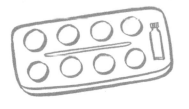

- 5 -
RAINBOW SCIENCE

Recognizing and identifying colors is one of the first things we teach our toddlers. It's an important early childhood concept. The best way to help your child learn is repeated exposure through play and identifying the colors you see all around!

This chapter provides plenty of opportunities to talk about colors. It is full of activities that explore color through experiments, activities, and art. Your child will build important neural connections by sorting, mixing, identifying, and observing. While they are at it, they will also be working on their fine motor skills and sensory exploration.

There will be a lot of colors coming at you in this chapter. We'll use all the colors of the rainbow: red, orange, yellow, green, blue, and purple. If this is too overwhelming for your toddler, feel free to cut back and focus on two or three colors at a time!

Colored Carnations

This is a simple watch-and-observe activity to show your toddler how water moves through a plant!

Messiness: 2
Prep time: None
Activity time: 5 minutes + wait time

MATERIALS

Clear cup

Water

Food coloring

Spoon

White carnation flower (or celery stalk with leaves)

STEPS

1. Fill the cup about halfway with water.

2. Put at least 10 drops of food coloring into the water.

3. Ask your child to mix it with a spoon.

4. Cut the stem of your flower (so it has a fresh cut) and put it into the water.

5. Ask your child what color the flower petals are. Ask what they think will happen.

6. Come back in a few hours and ask your child if they notice any differences.

7. Check on the flower the next day and ask your child if anything has changed. Don't forget to check the leaves and stems, too!

TIP *Use multiple cups with different colors of water to end up with different-colored flowers.*

Rainbow Rice

Dyeing rice is much easier than you might think. The colors turn out beautiful and your toddler can practice scooping and pouring to make a rainbow in a jar.

Messiness: 3
Prep time: None
Activity time: 10 minutes + drying time

MATERIALS

Uncooked white rice

Sealable bags

Vinegar

Food coloring, at least in primary colors: red, yellow, and blue

Wax paper

Bowls

Small cup

Funnel

Medium-size jar with lid

STEPS

1. Ask your toddler to help you pour 1 cup of uncooked rice into a sealable bag.

2. Add 1 teaspoon of vinegar and a few drops of food coloring. Use more if you want a deeper color.

3. Seal the bag and ask your toddler to shake it until the color is mixed thoroughly.

4. Pour the rice out of the bag onto a sheet of wax paper.

5. Repeat for the other colors and let the rice dry for a few hours.

6. Once dry, put the rice in different bowls for your child to scoop from.

7. Help your child layer different colors of rice in the jar using a small cup and funnel. Instant rainbow!

CAUTION! *Make sure your child knows this rice is not for eating.*

SKILLS
LEARNED

colors

fine motor
skills

hand-eye
coordination

classifying

matching

Let's Sort!

This simple activity focuses on the scientific skills of sorting and classifying. It is also a great way to practice fine motor skills and hand-eye coordination.

Messiness: 1
Prep time: **5 minutes**
Activity time: **15 minutes**

MATERIALS

Empty tall oatmeal container or potato chips can with lid

Hole puncher

Markers, in various colors

Binder hole reinforcement stickers (optional)

Pipe cleaners, in various colors

PREP

1. Punch one hole in the top of the container's lid for each color of pipe cleaner you have.

2. Using the markers, color a circle around each hole to match the colors of pipe cleaners. Or, if you have the binder hole stickers, stick one around each hole and color them in.

3. Put the lid on the container.

STEPS

1. Pick a pipe cleaner and ask your child which color hole it matches. Show them how to stick the pipe cleaner in the hole and push it all the way through.

2. Ask them to try with a different pipe cleaner.

3. When the pipe cleaners are all in, take off the lid and start again!

CAUTION! *Don't leave your child alone with pipe cleaners. Their centers are made of metal, and they can be pokey at the end. Pipe cleaners can also get bunched enough to be a choking hazard.*

Color Sticker Sort

Placing objects into different categories is a scientific skill. Peeling and sticking is a great activity to work on fine motor skills. This activity combines both!

Messiness: 1
Prep time: None
Activity time: 10 minutes

MATERIALS

Paper, in various colors (or use white paper and make a block of color at the top with a marker)

Tape (optional)

Solid-color dot stickers

STEPS

1. Tape each color of paper to a wall for a vertical activity, or lay them out on a flat surface like the floor or a table.

2. Peel one sticker off the sheet and model your thought process. Say, "I see this sticker is blue. I'm going to find the paper that is also blue and stick it on there."

3. Invite your child to try peeling a sticker and sticking it to the matching sheet of paper.

TIP *To make it easier for your toddler, peel the sticker border off so only the stickers remain. Then show them how to bend the sticker sheet so the sticker pops off enough for them to grab it.*

CAUTION! *Make sure your child knows stickers belong on paper and not in mouths or on walls. Adult supervision is required.*

Color Tunnels

This is a fun game that involves rolling a ball through colored tunnels. You can practice colors while also introducing the concepts of force and friction.

Messiness: 1
Prep time: 5 minutes
Activity time: 15 minutes

MATERIALS

Card stock, in various colors

Painter's tape

A smooth ball, such as a tennis ball or baseball

Foil crumpled up into a ball

PREP

1. Tape the long side of a piece of card stock to the floor. Card stock should be large enough to make a tunnel big enough to roll a ball through.

2. Bend the card stock so it makes a tunnel and tape the other side to the floor.

3. Repeat for the other colors randomly around the room.

STEPS

1. Sit on the floor and show your child how to gently roll the smooth ball on the floor. No throwing! Aim for a specific colored tunnel and see if you can get the ball through.

2. Hand your child the ball and call out a tunnel color for them to aim for. They can be up close at first, then move farther away as their aim improves.

3. Now hand your child the ball of foil and ask them to roll it into a tunnel. Talk about the differences between the two balls. Which ball rolls more smoothly? Which ball rolls farther?

4. Have your child push the ball gently and see how far it goes. Then push it harder to see how much farther it goes.

CAUTION! *Don't use small bouncy balls because those are a choking hazard.*

Round Rainbow

Watch color move before your eyes in this fascinating activity that just requires some candy and plain water!

Messiness: 2
Prep time: None
Activity time: 5 minutes

MATERIALS

White plate

Hard-shelled candy, in various colors (such as Skittles or M&M's)

Cup of warm water

STEPS

1. Ask your child to arrange the candy pieces in a circle on the plate so they touch one another. Make sure there are varied colors with no two like colors side by side. This is a good opportunity to practice patterns!

2. Slowly pour a small amount of warm water on the dish. The water should cover the candies halfway.

3. Watch and see what happens!

CAUTION! *If you let your child try a candy, make sure they don't put too many in their mouth at once. The candies can stick together and create a choking hazard.*

Milky Color Explosion

Toddlers will love the surprising result in this colorful experiment! All you need is food coloring, dish soap, and milk to make a color explosion!

Messiness: 2
Prep time: None
Activity time: 5 minutes

MATERIALS

Shallow dish or bowl

Milk (2 percent or whole)

Food coloring, in various colors

Cotton swab

Dish soap

STEPS

1. Pour enough milk into the dish or bowl to cover the bottom about ¼ inch deep.

2. Add a drop of food coloring to the center of the milk. Repeat with three more colors.

3. Dip the cotton swab in the dish soap or add a drop to the end of the swab.

4. Tell your child to watch the bowl as you stick the swab in the center of the color and hold it there for 5 to 10 seconds.

5. Take out the swab and invite your child to stick it back in the bowl in a new area. Help your child hold the swab in place.

TIP *Try to keep your child from stirring with the cotton swab. It will stop the effect. When you're all done, you can invite them to stir everything together.*

Water Colors

Easily "mix" colors without actually mixing them with this quick activity!

Messiness: 2
Prep time: None
Activity time: 5 minutes

MATERIALS

Water

Large glass bowl

Glass cup

Yellow and blue food coloring, plus other colors to repeat activity

Spoon

STEPS

1. Fill the large glass bowl about three-quarters full with water.

2. Fill the glass cup about halfway with water.

3. Add a few drops of yellow food coloring to the large bowl. Let your child stir it to mix.

4. Add a few drops of blue food coloring to the glass cup. Let your child stir it to mix.

5. Take the glass cup of blue water and set it in the bowl of yellow water. Take a look at the glass from the side. Ask your child what color the water is in the cup. If it's hard to see the new color (green), put the bowl where light shines through it.

6. Lift the glass out of the bowl. Ask your child what color it is now.

7. Dump out the jar and bowl and make a new set of colors. Use blue and red for purple or yellow and red for orange. I find that yellow and blue work best.

Fizzy Color Surprise

Hide a few drops of food coloring under a spoonful of baking soda. When your child drops vinegar on it, the color will come fizzing through.

Messiness: 3
Prep time: 5 minutes
Activity time: 5 minutes

MATERIALS

Food coloring or liquid watercolors, in various colors

Muffin pan

Baking soda

Vinegar

Cup or bowl

Medicine dropper or pipette

PREP

1. Put a few drops of food coloring or liquid water-colors in each cup in the muffin pan. Use a different color for each cup.

2. Put 1 tablespoon of baking soda in each compartment so it covers the food coloring.

3. Pour some vinegar in a cup or bowl for your child to easily access.

STEPS

1. Using the medicine dropper or pipette, show your child how to suck up some vinegar. If that's too difficult, you can do this part for them.

2. Have your child pick a cup in the muffin pan and squeeze the vinegar into it. Watch what happens!

3. Ask your child what color they see. If they don't know, use it as a teaching opportunity. "Look, I see the color red!"

4. Repeat with the rest of the muffin cups.

CAUTION! *Make sure your child understands vinegar is not for drinking.*

Frozen Paint Pops

Freeze paint on craft sticks for a fun frozen twist to traditional painting.

Messiness: 5
Prep time: 5 minutes +
6 hours freezing time
Activity time: 20 minutes

MATERIALS

Tempera paint, in
various colors

Ice cube tray

Water

Spoon

Craft sticks, cut in half

Paper or cardboard

PREP

1. Pour a different color of paint into each ice cube mold. Add a little water and stir. Try adding a few colors in the same mold. Just don't mix them up!

2. Put a craft stick in each ice cube mold. If your paint is not very thick, your stick might tilt a bit. This is okay.

3. Freeze for at least 6 hours or overnight.

STEPS

1. Once they're frozen, pop out the paints as you would ice cubes. Leave the tray accessible for storage during painting!

2. Lay out your paper or cardboard.

3. Invite your child to choose a color and use it to paint on the paper. What happens as they slide it across the paper? How does the paint change as it starts to melt?

TIP *This activity is all about the process, so let your child explore! It's okay if they move to finger painting or exploring the paint pops themselves.*

CAUTION! *Make sure your child knows these are not real ice pops and they are not okay to eat.*

Rainbow Trail

Watch in awe as two ends of a rainbow magically connect—over a paper towel bridge!

Messiness: 2
Prep time: 5 minutes
Activity time: 15 minutes

MATERIALS

1 paper towel, cut into a 4-by-8-inch rectangle

Washable markers, in various colors

2 clear cups

Water

PREP

1. Color a straight rainbow with the markers on both short ends of the paper towel. The rainbow should be about 1½ inches tall. Make sure to use lots of ink.

2. Fill up each cup with just barely enough water to reach the paper towel.

STEPS

1. Place the cups side by side on a table or counter.

2. Gently place one end of the paper towel in each cup so they make contact with the water. Watch the colors start to rise! It will take about 10 minutes for the colors to meet in the middle.

TIP *After the rainbow trail is complete, check back later to see what happens. Parts of the rainbow will start to turn white again as the ink dissolves.*

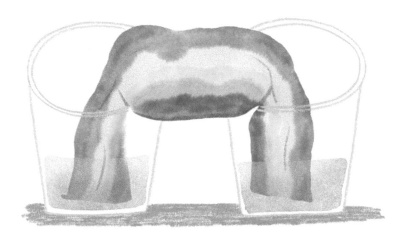

colors	physics	cause and effect	fine motor skills	SKILLS LEARNED

Rainbow Noisemaker

Let's make music with your very own colorful, rainbow-themed noisemaker! Explore your sense of sound and put on some music to shake to the beat!

Messiness: 1
Prep time: None
Activity time: 15 minutes

MATERIALS

Pony beads, in various colors

Pom-poms, in various colors

Empty water bottle

Hot glue

Hot glue gun

STEPS

1. Arrange the beads and pom-poms in front of your toddler.

2. Invite them to choose what they'd like to put in the bottle. Explain that the beads are added to make noise and the pom-poms are used for filler and to add color. Model how you select one item at a time and drop it in!

3. Every so often, put the lid on and give the bottle a shake to test out the sound. Stop filling the bottle when your child says so.

4. Put the lid on the bottle and use hot glue to secure it closed. Do this away from your child, since it is extremely hot. Let it dry.

5. Hand over the new musical shaker to your child and let them explore the sounds it makes. Ask them to shake it fast. Ask them to shake it slow. What does it sound like when you roll it on a flat surface? What does it sound like when you flip it over?

CAUTION! *Hot glue guns are extremely hot. Make sure it is plugged in in an area that your child cannot reach and will not be nearby.*

SKILLS
LEARNED

colors

classifying

physics

fine motor skills

matching

Rainbow Pom-Pom Drop

This science activity is about classifying colors, but with a vertical challenge to demonstrate gravity! Using tongs or fingers, your child can drop the pom-pom in the matching-colored tube and watch it come out the other end.

Messiness: 2
Prep time: 10 minutes
Activity time: 10 minutes

MATERIALS

Empty paper towel or toilet paper tubes

Paint, in various colors, and paintbrush; or paper, in various colors

Painter's tape

Sturdy foam board (optional)

Container or tray

Pom-poms, in various colors

Children's tweezers or tongs (optional)

PREP

1. Either paint each tube or wrap colored paper around each tube and tape it. There should be one for each color of the rainbow.

2. Tape the tubes vertically (just a few inches apart) on a wall or sturdy foam board (if using).

3. Pour the pom-poms into a container or onto a tray and set it near the tubes. Add tongs or tweezers if you have them.

STEPS

1. Show your child the tubes and ask them what they think will happen when you drop a pom-pom in.

2. Invite your child to pick out a pom-pom and drop it in the tube that matches. Ask them to tell you the color if they can. If not, then you can talk about what color it is. "Oh, you picked a blue one."

3. Your child can head back to the container for another color. Repeat until all pom-poms are sorted by color.

CAUTION! *Pom-poms could be a choking hazard.*

Sprinkle Dance

Your little scientist will use their voice to make the sprinkles dance. Just get close to the bowl and hum. Watch those sound waves make the sprinkles move!

Messiness: 2
Prep time: 5 minutes
Activity time: 5 minutes

MATERIALS

Bowl

Plastic wrap

Rubber band

Tray

Round sprinkles, in rainbow colors (they're lighter than the long ones)

PREP

Take a piece of plastic wrap and put it on top of the bowl. Secure it with a rubber band. Set it on the tray to help collect loose sprinkles.

STEPS

1. Invite your child to gently shake some sprinkles onto the top of the plastic wrap. (They easily bounce off and go everywhere.)

2. Ask your child if they know of a way to get the sprinkles to move without touching the bowl.

3. Show your child how to hum. Keep your lips closed but make noise in your throat.

4. Now tell your child to get close to the bowl with their mouth and hum. The sprinkles should start moving! If the sprinkles don't move, hum louder or get closer to the bowl, perhaps even touching it.

Find the Color

With just a piece of cardboard and a marker, you can make a search-and-find game for your toddler to get them moving and searching for colors to match—whether they are indoors or outside!

Messiness: 1
Prep time: 10 minutes
Activity time: 15 minutes

MATERIALS

Cardboard

Box cutter or scissors

Markers or paint, in various colors

Paintbrush (optional)

PREP

1. Cut a rectangle of cardboard from a box flap or the inside of a cereal or cracker box. It should be about 5 inches wide by 10 inches tall.

2. Cut a 3-inch-square window at the top of the cardboard.

3. Use the markers or paint to add a specific color underneath the window.

4. Repeat for all the colors you'd like to use.

STEPS

1. Hand your toddler one colored piece of cardboard. Ask them what color is on the bottom of the cardboard piece. If they don't know the color yet, tell them what color it is.

2. Show your toddler how you can hold up the cardboard to have something appear in the window.

3. Ask your toddler to go find something around the room that matches the color below the cutout window. Hold it up so it appears in the window to make sure it's a match.

4. Then go find something different that matches.

5. Switch the colored piece of cardboard if you made more, and repeat.

Explore Mixing Colors

Let your child learn about colors by mixing colored water. What new colors will they create?

Messiness: 3
Prep time: 5 minutes
Activity time: 10 minutes

MATERIALS

At least 4 clear glasses or jars

Water

Food coloring, in primary colors: red, yellow, and blue

Pipette, medicine dropper, or turkey baster

PREP

1. Fill all but one jar three-quarters full with water. Leave the remaining jar empty.

2. Add a few drops of food coloring to each jar of water—one color per jar to make red, yellow, and blue.

3. Arrange the colors next to one another in a line out on the grass or on a table, with the empty jar in the middle.

STEPS

1. Tell your child they are going to be a scientist today and practice making new colors.

2. Show them what you are using to suck up water (pipette, dropper, or baster) and how it works.

3. Invite them to pick a color, suck some up, and squirt it into the empty jar. Practice naming the color as they do this.

4. Then pick a different color and add it to the same jar. Can they name this color, too?

5. Ask your child what they noticed and what changed in the jar.

6. Dump the water out and pick two different colors to add together in the empty jar.

CAUTION! *Glass can break if dropped. Use plastic containers if you are worried your child may tip them over.*

Rainbow Tape Resist

Tape-resist painting is a process-focused art project that explores color and paint blocking. Tape your canvas and let your child go all out by painting with the colors of the rainbow. Their artwork is revealed when you remove the tape!

Messiness: 3
Prep time: 5 minutes
Activity time: 10 minutes

MATERIALS

Canvas or cardboard

Washi tape or masking tape

Paint, in rainbow colors

Paintbrush

PREP

Stick strips of tape across the canvas. The strips should cross each other randomly. Alternatively, you can create stripes.

STEPS

1. Hand your child the paintbrush and invite them to pick different colors to paint the different sections. Tell them to make sure all the white parts get covered. It doesn't matter if they paint over the tape or not. (The paint will not show where there is tape.)

2. Once the paint has dried, peel up one edge of the tape and have your toddler help you peel it all off to reveal their rainbow-colored artwork!

Make Colored Light!

Let's take colors off the paper and put them onto the walls with light! Your scientist will discover how to make colored light. You can also experiment with what happens when you mix two colors of light.

Messiness: 1
Prep time: **None**
Activity time: 10 minutes

MATERIALS

3 flashlights

White wall or white poster board

Cellophane, in red, blue, and green

3 rubber bands

STEPS

1. Take your flashlights, poster board (if using), and child into a dark room.

2. Give your child a flashlight and let them explore what color they see on the wall or poster board.

3. Cover each light with a different color of cellophane and use a rubber band to secure it to the flashlight. (You may need to turn the light back on for this.)

4. Hand a flashlight to your toddler and let them push the button to turn it on. Have them shine the light on the wall or poster board. What color do they see now?

5. Repeat with the other two flashlight colors.

CAUTION! *Make sure to tell your toddler we don't shine lights in other people's faces or our own eyes.*

SKILLS
LEARNED

colors

physics

fine motor
skills

measuring

Water Rainbow

Did you know that adding sugar to water changes its density, so you can stack colors and they won't mix? This is a great experiment to create a water rainbow in a jar.

Messiness: 3
Prep time: None
Activity time: 10 minutes

MATERIALS

4 clear glasses or jars

Warm water

Food coloring, in red, yellow, green, and blue

Spoon

Sugar

Measuring cups

Pipette or medicine dropper

Smaller, more narrow clear glass (like a shot glass or champagne glass)

STEPS

1. Fill the four larger glasses up with the same amount of water in each.

2. Add a few drops of food coloring to each glass to make red, yellow, green and blue. Ask your toddler to help stir.

3. Leave the red cup as is. Add ¼ cup of sugar to the yellow cup, ½ cup of sugar to the green, and 1 cup of sugar to the blue.

4. Stir to mix thoroughly and ask your toddler to help. This is important! You need the sugar to be fully dissolved. If it isn't, you can put the glass in the microwave for 20 seconds and stir again.

5. Take your dropper and suck up some blue water. Squeeze the blue water into the smaller glass. *Very important: Squeeze it super slowly onto the edge of the empty, narrow glass.* Repeat with the same color until you have a ½-inch layer in the glass.

6. Take your dropper and suck up some green water. *Very important: Squeeze it super slowly onto the edge of the narrow glass.* Repeat with the same color until you have a ½-inch layer in the glass.

7. Repeat with the yellow water and then the red water. You should see layers of color. Hold it up to the light for a better view!

TIP *You can start off with only two colors (one with no sugar and one with ½ cup sugar) to make it simpler. Your toddler can help suck up the water, but an adult needs to squeeze it into the new cup because it must be squeezed very slowly and gently against the edge of the glass.*

CAUTION! *Glass can break if dropped. If you are doing this experiment on a hard surface or are worried your child may tip the glasses over, you can use clear plastic containers instead.*

Rainbow Reflections

Do you have an old CD lying around? Grab it, a flashlight, and a piece of paper to explore some rainbow reflections!

Messiness: 1
Prep time: **None**
Activity time: **5 minutes**

MATERIALS

2 sheets of paper
(1 white, 1 black)

Flashlight

CD

STEPS

1. Turn off the lights and lay the white paper on a flat surface.

2. Ask your toddler to turn on the flashlight by pressing the button. Set the flashlight on the paper.

3. Hold the CD so the backside is facing the light and it is perpendicular to the paper. Twist it and change angles until you see a rainbow appear on your paper!

4. Swap the white paper for black paper. Find your rainbow again and see how it compares to the first rainbow. Is it darker or lighter?

Floating Rainbow Name

It's magical! Draw letters in different colors on a plate with dry-erase markers. Then add a bit of water and the letters will come to life and float around.

Messiness: 2
Prep time: 5 minutes
Activity time: 5 minutes

MATERIALS

Plate

Dry-erase markers, in various colors

Room-temperature water

Pitcher or measuring cup with a pouring spout

PREP

1. On a plate, write your child's name using different colors of dry-erase markers for each letter. Don't press too hard! Write as lightly as you can, so the letters have an easier time coming off.

2. Fill the pitcher with room-temperature water.

STEPS

1. Ask your child if they know what each letter is on the plate. Do they know what the letters spell? Ask them to name the colors, too. If they don't know, tell them each color. "This is the letter *H* and it is the color blue."

2. Tell your child to watch the letters and see what happens.

3. Slowly pour water at the edge of the plate (not on top of the letters) until there is a layer of water covering the plate.

4. Observe carefully and ask your child to tell you what they see happening! (Hint: The letters should lift off the plate and float around!)

TIP *If the letters don't come up, try again. The key is to write lightly and pour the water very slowly at the edge of the plate.*

- 6 -
WONDER OF WATER

Just add water.

That's an easy fix for a lot of things when it comes to little ones. Cranky toddler? Find a water activity. Are they feeling anxious, mad, or sad? It's water time! Whether it is through a bath or an activity, water really does help soothe and reset our emotions.

I am also a huge fan of simple, open-ended toys to help guide play. Many of the activities in this chapter just require basic items and water. That's it. These activities will allow your child to explore and be creative in their play!

This chapter also includes plenty of simple science investigations. They will get to explore concepts such as buoyancy, density, viscosity, displacement, and weather. But will they know that? Nope. Remember that it's all about the experience and observation at this age!

Wiggly Paper Towel Worms

When I was a kid, one of our waiting games at restaurants was to make worms from the straw wrappers and watch them grow as we dropped water on them. Well, you can make your own wiggly worms at home with paper towels!

Messiness: 2
Prep time: 5 minutes
Activity time: 5 minutes

MATERIALS

Paper towels

Markers

Pencil or
wooden dowel

Plate

Cup of water

Dropper or straw

PREP

1. Cut paper towels into 5-by-4-inch rectangles. You can add color to your paper towels using markers, if you choose.

2. Roll a paper towel rectangle tightly around the pencil or dowel. If you colored yours, have the color be on the inside when you roll it up.

3. Scrunch the top and bottom of the paper towel tightly toward each other.

4. Then take it off the pencil. Add a smiley face to one end.

5. Repeat for as many worms as you'd like to make.

STEPS

1. Arrange your paper towel worms on a plate.

2. Invite your child to fill up a dropper or straw with water. (If using a straw, put the straw in water and put your finger over the straw's top. Don't remove your finger until you are ready to drop the water out.)

3. Ask your child what they think will happen when water gets on a worm.

4. Have them release the water on a specific worm and watch what happens! (Hint: The worm will wiggle and grow! The color will reveal itself, too, if you colored the paper towel.)

5. Repeat for as many worms as you made!

Water Cycle in a Bag

This activity is a great visual to teach little learners about the water cycle. Put colored water in a bag and tape it to a window. Water droplets will condense on the bag to make "clouds," and when they get close enough or heavy enough, they will fall down the bag as "rain."

Messiness: 1
Prep time: 5 minutes
Activity time: 5 minutes + observation time

MATERIALS

Sealable plastic bag

Fine-point black marker

Water

Blue food coloring

Tape

Window

PREP

Draw the water cycle on the bag—waves of water on the bottom, wavy arrows on the left pointing up to a sun, a cloud next to the sun, and a cloud that is raining on the right.

STEPS

1. Ask your toddler to help fill the bag with a cup of water.

2. Put in a drop of blue food coloring and seal the bag.

3. Tape the bag to a window. Explain to your toddler that the sun is going to heat the water in the bag like it does the water on our planet. The sun makes the droplets rise up into the sky, but the real-life water droplets are so tiny that we don't even see them in the air. But for this activity, you will get to see them! *Be very careful not to touch the bag once it's up.* Just watch and wait patiently.

4. Come back in a few hours to see if any water droplets have formed on the inside walls of the bag. Explain that the water droplets in the sky collect together to make clouds.

5. When the cloud gets filled with water droplets, they will release back down to the ground as rain!

6. Keep watching your bag over the next day to see when water droplets start to fall down the bag. It's raining! (Don't expect it to be fast like rain, though. You may just see a drop every so often.)

Exploring Water Displacement

Your little scientist will observe where water goes when you put something in the cup with it. They are learning about volume by just seeing what happens!

Messiness: 2
Prep time: 5 minutes
Activity time: 5 minutes

MATERIALS

2 clear cups or jars

Water

Heavy and lighter (but still sinkable) items, such as rocks, clementines, eggs, ice, and beads

Dry-erase marker or tape

PREP

Fill both cups of water to the same level (about halfway) and gather your heavy and light items.

STEPS

1. Put the cups of water in front of your child and ask them to mark the water level (either with a dry-erase marker or the top of a piece of tape) on each cup.

2. Ask your child what they think will happen when you drop something heavy in the cup.

3. Invite them to gently set the heavy object in one of the cups and watch what happens to the water.

4. Mark the new water line with the dry-erase marker or tape.

5. Now hold up a lighter item and ask them if they think the water will move up again. Will it be more or less than the first item?

6. Ask them to gently set it in the other cup and watch what happens to the water. Did it move up at all? Try adding a few more of the same item.

7. Keep adding objects in both cups to see how far you can get the water to go up!

CAUTION! *Some items may be choking hazards.*

Floating Egg

How do you make an egg float? By adding salt! This activity will demonstrate how salt changes the density of the water, making the egg more buoyant and causing it to float.

Messiness: 2
Prep time: None
Activity time: 5 minutes

MATERIALS

2 clear cups or jars

2 eggs

Salt

Spoon

STEPS

1. Fill the cups halfway with water.

2. Ask your child to gently drop an egg into one of the cups. Did the egg sink or float?

3. Then invite your child to dump a lot of salt into the other cup of water. They can pour as much as they would like, but aim for at least ½ cup.

4. Have your child stir it well with a spoon.

5. Ask them to gently drop the other egg into the cup of salt water. Did the egg sink or float?

6. To make a real-world connection, explain that it is easier for people to float in salt water like the ocean than it is in fresh water!

Sink or Float?

Your child will learn about density by exploring which objects sink and which objects float in water.

Messiness: 2
Prep time: 5 minutes
Activity time: 5 minutes

MATERIALS

Objects that will sink, such as coins, rocks, forks, and toy figures

Objects that will float, such as oranges, sticks, leaves, corks, and plastic blocks

Bowl or container

Water

PREP

Collect your items and fill the bowl with water.

STEPS

1. Ask your child to choose an item and drop it in the bowl. Does it sink or float?

2. Ask them to pick another item. Again, talk about how it sinks or floats.

3. Repeat with other items. Once you've had examples of an object sinking and floating, ask your child to guess what will happen before they drop an item in the bowl.

4. Have your child go collect a few more things around the house to see if the objects will sink or float.

TIP *Once you find out that the orange floats, peel it. Then drop it back in the water to find it sinks!*

CAUTION! *The items you drop in may be choking hazards.*

Appearing Pictures

Amaze your toddler by making pictures magically appear by dropping two paper towels in water.

Messiness: 2
Prep time: 5 minutes
Activity time: 5 minutes

MATERIALS

Paper towels

Markers (A fine-point permanent marker will stay put, while a water-based marker will start to bleed and make the water inky.)

Baking dish

Water

PREP

1. Fold a paper towel in half.

2. Open it like a book and draw a picture with colored markers on the inside right-hand page.

3. Fill a baking dish up with about an inch of water.

STEPS

1. Hand the paper towel to your child with the top layer covering your picture, like a closed book.

2. Invite your child to drop the paper towel into the water and watch the picture appear (don't look away, it's quick!).

3. It's pretty amazing, so you might need to draw a few more pictures to satisfy your toddler saying, "Do it again!"

SKILLS
LEARNED

observation

cause and
effect

problem-
solving

sensory
development

botany

Frozen Nature Treasures

Your toddler will love to see bits of nature frozen into blocks of ice for them to explore. They can experiment with different ways to try to break them free—for example, by melting or breaking the ice.

Messiness: 2

Prep time: 5 minutes +
6 hours freezing time

Activity time: 20 minutes

MATERIALS

Items from nature, such as flower petals or leaves

Muffin pan or silicone ice tray

Water

Wooden mallet, squirt bottle, cup, or larger bowl of water (optional)

Tray (optional)

PREP

1. Place the nature items in the muffin pan.

2. Add water to cover the items.

3. Put in the freezer for at least 6 hours or overnight.

STEPS

1. Remove the ice blocks from the pan and set the nature treasures on a tray or out on the grass.

2. Ask your child to try to get the nature items out of the ice.

3. Watch your child experiment and problem-solve without helping them. You can have some tools they may use nearby, such as a wooden mallet for hammering, or a squirt bottle or cup for pouring water and melting the ice.

Paint the Sidewalk—with Water!

You don't need paint or chalk to be artistic on the sidewalk. Sure, your picture may not stay for long, but it is fun to watch it disappear. This is a great activity when you just need something simple!

Messiness: 2
Prep time: None
Activity time: 10 minutes

MATERIALS

Cup of water

Paintbrush

STEPS

1. Take your cup of water and paintbrush outside to a concrete area.

2. Invite your child to dip the paintbrush in the water and paint a picture on the sidewalk.

3. Keep an eye on your child's first strokes and watch as the water begins to evaporate away. (If you want this step to happen quickly, do this activity in the sun. If you want the activity to last longer, do it in the shade.) Point out to your toddler what's happening. Explain that the water is drying up. You can even use bigger words like *evaporating into the air*!

4. Practice painting shapes, letters, and numbers, or just have fun with scribbles and pictures!

SKILLS
LEARNED

chemistry

fine motor
skills

hand-eye
coordination

observation

Pour Water with a String

How can you pour water into a cup a foot away without making a mess? The trick is a string! This is such a cool thing for your toddler to watch (and for adults, too!).

Messiness: 2
Prep time: None
Activity time: 5 minutes

MATERIALS

Measuring cup with a pour spout

Water

Food coloring

Spoon

Piece of cotton string or twine, cut to 18 inches (needs to be absorbent and thicker than thread)

Cup

STEPS

1. Fill the measuring cup with water.

2. Add a few drops of food coloring and ask your toddler to help stir it to mix.

3. Put the string in the water and submerge and soak it for about 10 seconds.

4. Keep one end of the string in the measuring cup where the spout is, and put the other end in the empty cup.

5. Tell your toddler it's their job to hold the cup on the table or counter steady while you pour.

6. Lift the measuring cup in the air and far enough away from your toddler's cup so the string is diagonal. (You will have to hold the string with your finger so it doesn't fall out.)

7. *Slowly* begin to pour the water out and watch what happens. (Hint: The water will stay on the string and pour into the empty cup!) Expect to see a few drops on the counter, so make sure to do this in an area that can get wet and that the food coloring won't stain.

8. Try to pour the water back into the measuring cup now!

SKILLS
LEARNED

physics

observation

fine motor
skills

Soak & Squish

Your toddler will investigate sponges with this water play activity. Soak up water and where does it all go? Squeeze it out and there it is! This activity is great for strengthening those hand muscles, too.

Messiness: **3**
Prep time: **None**
Activity time: **15 minutes**

MATERIALS

2 medium-size tubs or large bowls

Water

Kitchen or car-wash sponges

STEPS

1. Fill up one tub with water.

2. Show your child a sponge and ask them to hold it and feel it. Does it feel soft or hard? Is it light or heavy?

3. Ask your child to set the sponge on the water. Does it sink or float?

4. Have your child dunk the sponge under the water and bring it back up. How does it feel now? Is it soft or hard? Light or heavy?

5. Now for the fun part: Hold the sponge over the second empty tub and squeeze it! What happens?

6. Ask your child if they can get all the water from the first tub into the new one by just using the sponge.

CAUTION! *Sponges can rip apart into small pieces, which could be a choking hazard.*

Build a Boat

It's problem-solving time! Work with your toddler to create a boat that floats. You can use foil, fruit peels, or craft sticks.

Messiness: 3
Prep time: None
Activity time: 10 minutes

MATERIALS

Items to make a boat, such as aluminum foil, craft sticks, or fruit peels

Glue or rubber bands (optional)

A bowl of water

Toy figure

STEPS

1. Ask your toddler to help you make a boat that really floats.

2. Devise a plan. Talk to your toddler about what makes a good boat (for example, it floats, doesn't let water in it, and can hold a person).

3. Get to work creating a boat with the materials you have. If you use craft sticks, you will need glue or rubber bands to hold them together.

4. Have your toddler help you test the boat by putting it in a bowl of water. Does it float? The final test is to add a toy figure to see if the boat can hold its weight and still float.

CAUTION! *Never leave your toddler unattended near water.*

Squirt, Squirt!

My kids loved this activity because a spray bottle is just so much fun to spray. It also strengthens their hands for fine motor control, and you can make it into a learning game!

Messiness: 2
Prep time: **None**
Activity time: 10 minutes

MATERIALS

Spray bottle

Water

Toys that can get wet

Sidewalk chalk, in various colors (optional)

STEPS

1. Fill the spray bottle with water.

2. Set up the toys on the ground (in an area that can get wet).

3. Show your child how to squeeze the trigger of the squirt bottle to get water to spray out.

4. Ask them if they can squirt a specific toy. Repeat with the names of other toys.

5. If they know colors, shapes, numbers, or letters, draw or write them on the sidewalk with chalk.

6. Call out a specific color, shape, etc., and have your child go to it and spray it. Repeat until they have sprayed them all.

CAUTION! *Make sure to explain to your child that you never spray someone in the face or turn the spray bottle around on yourself.*

Musical Jars

Your toddler will make music with jars of water! Fill them with various amounts of water and observe the different sounds you can make by tapping them with a spoon.

Messiness: 2
Prep time: 5 minutes
Activity time: 10 minutes

MATERIALS

5 glass jars or cups

Water

Metal spoon

PREP

Fill the jars with a different amount of water in each and set them in a row in front of your child.

STEPS

1. Model how you tap the spoon on the side of the jar.

2. Tap on a different jar and ask your child if that sound was higher or lower than the first sound.

3. Hand over the spoon and invite your child to explore the sounds of all the jars.

CAUTION! *Since glass is breakable, it's best to do this activity on a soft surface, like grass or a blanket on the ground, where the jars won't break if they get knocked over.*

Pepper Scatter

This activity explores surface tension. Your toddler will delight in watching the pepper scatter away from their finger as if it's afraid!

Messiness: 2
Prep time: None
Activity time: 5 minutes

MATERIALS

Shallow bowl,
or pie pan

Water

Black pepper

Dish soap

Plate (optional)

STEPS

1. Fill the shallow bowl with water to cover the bottom.

2. Let your child sprinkle pepper all over the water. You want to add enough flakes so that they're visible and cover different areas of the water.

3. Squirt some dish soap on your child's finger or put the soap on a plate and have your child dip their finger into it.

4. Have your child stick their finger in the pepper water and *hold still*. Don't look away, because the reaction's quick! Watch the pepper scatter away from their finger.

5. Ask your child to remove their finger *without mixing* if they want to try it again.

6. Get more dish soap and have them stick their finger back in. Does it happen again?

Ice Painting

Let's change up the canvas by painting a frozen ice block. This is a great activity for a hot summer day, but it's also fun in winter for a snow or ice theme. Explore what the colors do when they mix together on the watery surface.

Messiness: 4
Prep time: 5 minutes +
6 hours freezing time
Activity time: 15 minutes

MATERIALS

Containers to freeze water in

Water

Tray or baking dish, for catching puddles

Watercolors, in various colors

Paintbrush

PREP

Fill your containers with water and put them in the freezer for at least 6 hours or overnight.

STEPS

1. Get your ice blocks from the freezer and remove them from the containers.

2. Set the ice blocks on your tray or in a baking dish.

3. Invite your child to start painting.

4. Ask them what they notice about the colors and how they change as the ice melts. What happens when colors mix?

Ice Fishing

Scooping and transferring are important skills a toddler needs to practice! Make it a game by letting them fish for ice while exploring the science of different states of water.

Messiness: **4**
Prep time: **None**
Activity time: **20 minutes**

MATERIALS

Pitcher

Water

Smaller storage container

Larger storage container

Ice

Slotted spoon

STEPS

1. Fill the pitcher up with water and ask your child to help you pour the water into the smaller container. Continue until your container is filled with water.

2. Put the small container inside the large container.

3. Add plenty of ice to the smaller container. Ask your toddler if the ice sinks or floats. Explain how ice is solid and is frozen water. Water is a liquid!

4. Take the slotted spoon and model how your toddler can scoop up an ice cube and drop it into the area of the large container surrounding the small container.

5. Hand the spoon over and tell your toddler to give it a try.

6. Keep scooping until all the ice is transferred to the dry area.

7. If the ice isn't melted yet, put the ice back in the water and do it again!

physics

observation

language
development

SKILLS
LEARNED

The Magic Water Glass

This activity is as easy as can be. Your toddler needs a front row seat to watch as the arrows behind the glass change direction as it fills up with water! They will also be able to see how water acts as a magnifying glass.

Messiness: 1
Prep time: 5 minutes
Activity time: 5 minutes

MATERIALS

Marker

Card stock, poster board, or cardboard

Clear glass

Pitcher of water

PREP

On the piece of card stock, draw an arrow the width of your glass, about 2 inches from the bottom, pointing left or right. Draw another arrow a few inches above the first arrow going the opposite direction. Make sure it is not above the top of the glass. The goal is to have both arrows in view within the glass when you are looking through it.

STEPS

1. Place the card stock against something so it stands vertically.

2. Put the glass in front of the card stock so you can see both arrows when looking through it.

3. Invite your toddler to have a seat in front of the cup and ask them to point which way the bottom arrow is pointing.

4. Fill the cup up with water until it's just past the first arrow. Ask your toddler what way the arrow is pointing now!

5. Ask your toddler which arrow looks bigger now.

6. Continue to fill the glass up with water until it is above the top arrow. Ask your toddler which way that arrow is pointing now!

7. Slide the glass away from the card stock and watch as the arrows turn back the other way!

Pencil Poke

You'd think when you poke a hole in a bag of water with a pencil that it would leak. But not if you have the pencil go through both sides and keep the pencil there! You likely have all the materials nearby, so go and surprise your toddler with this simple activity.

Messiness: 2
Prep time: None
Activity time: 5 minutes

MATERIALS

Sealable plastic bag

Water

Sharpened pencils

STEPS

1. Fill the plastic bag halfway with water and seal it.

2. Have your toddler hold it in the air. Ask what they think will happen when you poke the pencil through the bag.

3. Jab a sharpened pencil through both sides of the bag (but make sure to leave the pencil in or you will have leaks!).

4. Invite your toddler to try pushing a pencil through (do it outside or over a sink just in case).

5. Take a look at the pencils and bag up close. Notice that the plastic seems to be sealing itself around the pencil.

6. Continue with as many pencils as you'd like! Make sure you're over a sink when it's time to pull them out.

CAUTION! *Pencils are sharp objects.*

Tornado Watch

Create your own little tornado in a jar to watch in the safety of your home!

Messiness: 1
Prep time: None
Activity time: 5 minutes

MATERIALS

Glass jar with lid

Water

Hand sanitizer or dish soap

STEPS

1. Ask your toddler to help you pour water into the jar up to the neck.

2. Add a squirt of hand sanitizer or dish soap. (Dish soap can turn the water murky if you add too much or spin it often.)

3. Put the lid on the jar.

4. Hold the jar but keep it on the counter. Move it quickly in a circular pattern to get the water swirling. Ask your toddler what they see! (Hint: It's a tornado!)

5. Spin the jar again to keep it going or let your toddler give it a try.

CAUTION! *Make sure you do this activity in an area where the jar won't break if it's dropped.*

How Fast Does It Fall?

Your scientist will explore the viscosity of different fluids in this experiment by seeing how long it takes an object to fall to the bottom of the glass.

Messiness: 2
Prep time: None
Activity time: 10 minutes

MATERIALS

A clear glass for every item you test (they should be the same size)

Water

Hair gel (optional)

Honey (optional)

Corn syrup (optional)

Dish soap (optional)

Cooking oil (optional)

Items that will sink in water, such as coins and beads (the item needs to be the same throughout: 6 pennies, 6 beads, etc.)

STEPS

1. Line your glasses up and ask your toddler to help you pour the liquids (water, hair gel, honey, corn syrup, dish soap, and cooking oil) into separate glasses. There should be at least 2 inches of liquid in each glass. You don't have to use every liquid on the list, but make sure to have at least one glass filled with water and another glass with a thicker fluid.

2. Hold the item you're going to sink just over the water. (If it's a coin, hold it so the circular side will fall first.) Ask your toddler to help you count to see how long it takes for the item to get to the bottom.

3. Drop the item in the water and start counting—this is a quick one!

4. Have your child drop the item in the second glass and start counting. Watch the item fall through the fluid. Is it faster than the water or slower?

5. Continue with each remaining glass and compare the results. Which fluid was the thickest and took the longest for the item to get through? Which fluid was the thinnest and took the item the least amount of time to get through?

CAUTION! *The items you drop in may be choking hazards.*

SKILLS
LEARNED

weather

observation

language
development

Shaving Cream Rain Cloud

Toddlers will love this activity that helps them learn where rain comes from. The shaving cream acts as the cloud, and you'll see the food coloring make its way down as the rain.

Messiness: 2
Prep time: None
Activity time: 5 minutes

MATERIALS

Clear glass

Water

Shaving cream

Blue food coloring

STEPS

1. Fill the glass about three-quarters full with water.

2. Squirt a layer of shaving cream in the glass. Don't make it more than about an inch thick or it will take too long for the food coloring to fall through the shaving cream. Tell your toddler the shaving cream is the rain cloud.

3. Invite your toddler to squeeze a few drops of blue food coloring on top of the shaving cream. Tell your toddler the food coloring is the water in the air/cloud.

4. Watch as the "rain" starts to fall out of the "cloud" and toward the ground. Explain to your child that the rain is falling from the cloud.

Resources

ACTIVITY PRINTABLES

Find printable resources at QuietBookQueen.com/blogs/this-and-that
/toddler-science-book-resources for the following activities:

- Sound Search (page 23)
- Nature Collection (page 30)
- Nature Scavenger Hunt (page 32)

CHILDREN'S BOOKS

» General Science

Scientist, Scientist, Who Do You See? by Chris Ferrie

This is a fun twist on the classic *Brown Bear, Brown Bear* story, where your child
will become acquainted with famous scientists.

What Is Science? by Rebecca Kai Dotlich

This rhyming book is the perfect introduction to science for a toddler. It explains
how science is all around us, like in the stars and rocks.

Ada Twist, Scientist by Andrea Beaty

This wonderful rhyming tale is about a little girl who is always wondering and
asking questions.

ABCs of Science by Chris Ferrie

A is for *amoeba*, *B* is for *bond*, *C* is for *conductor*. This board book introduces
science concepts at a very basic level.

» Color

Mix It Up! by Hervé Tullet

This wonderful interactive book instructs your toddler to tap and rub spots so they change on the next page.

Brown Bear, Brown Bear, What Do You See? by Bill Martin Jr. and Eric Carle

Children love the repetition in this book, and it is great for introducing colors. The companion book *Polar Bear, Polar Bear, What Do You Hear?* would be great to read before doing the Sound Search found on page 23.

» Nature

We're Going on a Leaf Hunt by Steve Metzger

In this book, children go on a walk during the fall and find leaves from different trees, while also running into obstacles they can't go over or under.

Some Bugs by Angela DiTerlizzi

This is a great book for helping toddlers discover bugs and what they do! Bring it along when you try Bug Study (page 25).

A Way with Wild Things by Larissa Theule

This would be a great story to read along with the activities Bug Study (page 25) and What's in the Grass? (page 41).

» Weather

All About Weather: A First Weather Book for Kids by Huda Harajli

This would be a great book to read before trying the Shaving Cream Rain Cloud (page 146) or Water Cycle in a Bag (page 124).

Little Cloud by Eric Carle

This is the perfect book to read before you settle down to do Cloud Pictures on page 22. It will really get the imagination going!

Water: Up, Down, and All Around by Natalie M. Rosinsky

This book breaks down the water cycle and would be wonderful to read before doing Water Cycle in a Bag on page 124.

Over and Under the Snow by Kate Messner

This story takes a look at what is happening under a layer of snow on the ground. Some animals are awake and keeping busy, while others are sleeping deeply in hibernation. Read it before making Sensory Snow on page 51!

WEBSITES

Little Pine Learners LittlePineLearners.com

The Dad Lab TheDadLab.com

Raising Dragons RaisingDragons.com

References

Center on the Developing Child (Harvard University). "InBrief: The Science of Early Childhood Development." Accessed October 9, 2020. DevelopingChild .Harvard.edu/resources/inbrief-science-of-ecd.

Yogman, Michael, Andrew Garner, Jeffrey Hutchinson, Kathy Hirsh-Pasek, and Roberta Michnick Golinkoff. "The Power of Play: A Pediatric Role in Enhancing Development in Young Children." *Pediatrics* 142, no. 3 (September 1, 2018): e20182058. doi.org/10.1542/peds.2018-2058.

Index

T

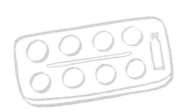

Acknowledgments

I'd like to thank Callisto Media for this opportunity to get screen-free activity ideas in the hands of so many families! I also have so much gratitude for my husband, kids, and family, who have supported me since the beginning of my business, back when it was just a "let's try it and see how it goes" idea. I would not be where I am today without their help in all other areas of life! And to my kids, you make me so proud. I love to watch your creativity and curiosity. Keep exploring and wondering!

About the Author

Kailan Carr is a former teacher and lives in California with her husband and two children. She earned her master's degree in education in literacy and has a reading specialist credential. Kailan started Quiet Book Queen & Crafts in Between (QuietBookQueen.com) to help parents and grandparents provide screen-free activities for their little ones. Quiet Book offers several hands-on activities in one place to develop fine motor skills and promote learning through play—at home or on the go! She has options for both people who sew and those who don't! She also wrote a paper-and-pencil activity book called *Ocean Animals Preschool Activity Book*. Follow her on Instagram at @QuietBookQueen or on Facebook at Facebook.com/quietbookqueen.

Printed in the USA
CPSIA information can be obtained
at www.ICGtesting.com
CBHW050304010624
9309CB00004B/11

9 781648 766435